Basic Financial Management

Revised Edition

Curtis W. Symonds

amacom

A Division of American Management Associations

Library of Congress Cataloging in Publication Data

Symonds, Curtis W
  Basic financial management.

  A revision of the 1969 ed. with addition of the author's Managing profits under inflation, first published separately in 1974.

  Includes index.
  1. Corporations—Finance. I. Title.
HG4026.S88   1978   658.1'5   78-6691
ISBN 0-8144-5481-X
ISBN 0-8144-7563-9

© 1969, 1974, 1978 AMACOM

A division of American Management Associations, New York.

First AMACOM paperback edition 1981.

Fourth Printing

Preface

THE concept of *profit management* as the total integration of volume, price, cost, and investment is fast emerging as the "survival kit" for business in a world of continuing inflation and economic uncertainty.

The revision of this book therefore finds the fundamentals completely unchanged, with alterations in the original text confined to an updating of values, a clarification of terms, and, in some instances, a more precise definition of various measurements.

The major change will be found in the addition of three new chapters that deal with managing profits under inflation. Originally published by AMACOM as a limited edition *Management Briefing* in 1974 and now no longer available as a separate publication, its inclusion in the revised edition of *Basic Financial Management* now adds this basic ingredient to the fundamentals of financial management.

Curtis W. Symonds

Contents

1

The Role of
Financial Management

FINANCIAL management is usually associated with the practice of accounting. As such, it is often regarded as the specialized function of the treasurer, controller, or other chief financial officer of the company. Since it deals with numerical values, it is also thought of in terms of budgets and forecasts, of balance sheets and profit and loss statements, or of tax returns and annual reports. To the uninitiated, it may represent a highly complex and specialized *function* of the business which acts as both scorekeeper and watchdog over the corporate finances. In many companies, it may even seem somewhat remote from the center of activity or detached from the mainstream of operating decisions. It is seldom regarded as the entire focal point or basic objective of the enterprise.

Financial management has been relegated to this position for two principal reasons. The first is the frequent lack of communication on the part of those who have direct responsibility for the financial affairs of the company. To the extent that they have turned inward to the language of accounting or have directed their reports to the needs of a system rather than to the needs of business, they have failed to assume a full partnership in management or to make the broader use of financial management and control a vital part of business operations. The second and perhaps more cogent reason lies in the individual manager's view of himself as a manager.

The Role of Management

In recent years, the role of management in business has gradually changed from the concept of a job to the level of a profession. In making the transition, the present-day manager has largely discarded the image of himself as a specialist in charge of a particular function and has moved instead into the more abstract realm of what has been called *professional management*. No longer concerned solely with the more prosaic problems of managing sales or production, the professional manager has taken on the new dimensions of the management sciences. He has learned, for example, the principles of organization, delegation of authority, planning and controlling, and he has developed a growing awareness of the behavioral sciences in his management of people. In short, he has been trained to organize and direct the specialized talents of others and has become highly mobile in the sense that he may now move easily from one industry to another. Confident and competent in the outward forms of management, he may be equally at home in sales or in production and may often assume responsibility for both.

This transition in the art or the science of management has seemingly carried with it the strong impression that the form and the substance of management are one and the same. What should managers manage? If the aim were still the management of individual functions, then it might be assumed that the management of sales, the management of production, or the management of research and engineering constituted an end objective in itself. If, on the other hand, the ability to organize, to delegate, to plan, to control, and to evaluate describes the manager's role, it must follow that the procedures themselves are both a means and an end.

While management will obviously not subscribe to such oversimplified conclusions or faulty interpretations of the manager's function, it rarely offers anything definitive in their place. In other words, it fails to provide the necessary focal point around which the basic aims and objectives of the manager can be centered— the focus which will give both meaning and substance to the task. It does not, for example, consistently provide a common ground or an integrated objective for each of the several functions or activities to be found in most business operations. While it may be obvious that technology has no value unless it can produce, that production is worthless unless it can be sold, and that sales are of little importance unless they are profitable, it is not as obvious that these functions will often tend to go their separate ways subject only to administration and management coordination.

The role of financial management is to unify these objectives and to give a common ground and a common purpose to each of these separate functions. On the single assumption that the business itself is profit-oriented and therefore operates under a free-enterprise system, such a basic purpose does exist and can be defined. *Managers should manage invested capital.*

At first glance, such a proposition might appear to suggest that all managers become experts in the field of accounting and finance or that the overall goals of management be confined to the structure of the corporate balance sheet. Taken in its broadest sense, however, the management of invested capital will be seen as the management of profit, since profit itself must be defined as an adequate return on capital employed. Once this fundamental goal has been recognized and accepted by management, the profit goal will be found to be quickly translatable into a series of subgoals for sales and production, for volume and price, and for investment and cost. These goals, in turn, will determine the structure of product and product-line relationships and the balancing of cost and investment. They will, in fact, provide the orchestration for each separate facet of the operation.

The intent is not to transform the average manager into a financial expert, or to ignore the role of the specialist, or to put a dollar sign on the value and dignity of the individual. It is quite the opposite. Properly used and properly understood, the concept of financial management will provide working tools in the hands of the specialist which will define his contribution to the business structure. Properly used, it will provide a clear choice of alternatives to the generalist in the middle levels of management who must guide the decisions of operational control. At the top of the management structure, it will increase the visibility required in strategic and long-range planning. It will, in short, provide a sense of direction within recognizable parameters that will permit consistent and coordinated action by management at all levels of operation.

Financial Management in a Small Company

The working concept of financial management is perhaps best understood by the owner-manager of the small business enterprise. Since he has total responsibility for the success or failure of the business, he is made keenly aware of the amount of capital employed to finance his operations, the cost of obtaining additional capital, and the use to which the capital is put. If the operation is one of job-shop production, for example, his approach to pricing will result in a quotation which not only provides for estimated costs of material, labor, and overhead marked up to provide a normal profit, but which will take into account any additional tie-up of capital that may be needed to carry heavier inventories or to finance longer-term receivables. While he may not be thinking in terms of such financial measurements as the cost of capital or the desired net profit return on average capital employed, he is instinctively dealing with the proper *elements* of financial management.

By increasing the quoted price to cover the interest cost of the money he will have to borrow to finance the expected increase in inventory, he is, for example, neglecting a risk factor which should dictate an even higher charge for the cost of funds employed. But whether or not his calculations are precise or even adequate, he has performed the important management function of recognizing the interdependence of cost and investment and the interrelationship of profit and capital. He has established as his own benchmark the fact that a profit of $100 on an investment of $1,000 is not of equal value with the same $100 profit on an investment of only $500, and his quoted price will reflect the difference.

Financial Management in a Large Company

By contrast, the professional manager of a unit in a large decentralized operation is at a distinct disadvantage. He is often isolated from the financial nerve center of the business and may have only a remote knowledge of the corporate use of capital or the impact his decisions may have on the size and cost of the funds employed. Since his horizons are normally limited to the boundaries of his particular function or functions, he is often forced to operate within the limits of his delegated authority and responsibility *without any clearly defined objectives.*

True, he may usually be limited by budgets and schedules which have been established for his area of control, or he may find his operating targets adjusted from time to time to meet the changing needs of the business. But within these rather limited objectives he may frequently find his own actions and decisions at variance with those of the connecting functions he is attempting to serve. Lacking overall direction on coordinated financial objectives, he adjusts instead to a series of fragmented targets and goals which may often work to the detriment of the overall desired results.

If, for example, the divisional sales manager of a large multidivision company is faced with a pricing decision that is expected to have a substantial effect on unit volume, he must, at best, *coordinate* his action with his counterpart in production. In a typical situation, such coordination might be limited to a simple checking on available productive capacity, on the lead time required for the procurement of parts and raw materials, or on estimated delivery dates based on the manufacturing cycle. Little attention may be given at the time to such related matters as the effect of the volume change on projected cost or the effect on capital funds required to finance increased payrolls or higher inventories.

If the pricing decision is also coupled with a decision to increase the level of finished goods stocked in the field warehouses, the situation may be even further aggravated by increasing investment at a faster rate than the dollar volume of sales or by increasing total cost beyond the level of incremental profit. Unaware of the total impact of such decisions and lacking guidelines which might specify the degree to which one move should be balanced against another, the sales manager might conceivably combine these two actions with a third and proceed to offer more liberal terms and conditions of sale.

Although this latter step would clearly increase the tie-up of funds in accounts receivable, no connecting link has been formed to measure the impact of such a change or even to associate the idea of added investment with that of added cost. And yet such unilateral decisions are by no means unique, particularly if the general management of the company is heavily sales-oriented, or if the normal profit-leverage for the business is found in the marketplace rather than in the research laboratory or in the manufacturing shop. The evidence appears in the reports of many firms whose sales have increased steadily year after year, but whose overall performance in terms of return on invested capital has, for some reason, shown a steady erosion of earning power.

Ineffectual "Controls"

The isolation of such decisions is by no means confined to the area of sales management, although the examples cited are both frequent and commonplace. Instances will be found at the manufacturing or divisional management level where inventories, for example, have been budgeted at a fixed dollar level of investment in accordance with planned levels of sales and production volume. In such cases, an original relationship has been established during the planning process between the level of investment and the level of volume it is intended to support.

Oftentimes, however, control is then subsequently exercised independently over the dollars committed to inventory—*without regard to changing levels of volume.* The full coordination and integration of financial management is lacking, and such "controls" eventually prove to be self-defeating.

The single area where most companies make a serious attempt at a completely integrated financial evaluation of proposals appears to lie in the more formal approach given to requests for capital investments in fixed assets. These are normally prepared on a prescribed form which calls for a description of the equipment to be purchased, its estimated cost and useful life, and a statement of alternatives. The estimated savings in material, in labor, or in overhead cost are shown in some detail as justification for the acquisition; they are then translated into measurements of *return on investment* and *cash payback* to indicate the relative merits of several different proposals. The more sophisticated approaches also add a measure of *discounted cash flow* in recognition of the time value of money and the total cost of capital employed. In form, the analysis required by such authorization requests is excellent. In practice, many of them suffer from the same attitudes or lack of financial integration that appears to be prevalent in decisions concerning inventories, accounts receivable, and so on.

The form is excellent in that it provides for a balancing of projected profit gain against projected investment and measures not only the expected total return on the funds invested but the *rate* at which it will be realized. All the factors are present and all the measurements are valid, yet postexpenditure audits reveal that the indicated targets are seldom met. The weakness in practice cannot be attributed to a lack of input data, to faulty arithmetic, or even to consistently poor estimates. The weakness will more probably be found in the question of management attitudes—attitudes which carry over from other segments of the operation.

Most companies, for example, do not require such a formal analysis or written authorization to permit increases or additions to the working capital elements of the business. Many managers who apparently have free rein to add $100,000 to inventory or $500,000 in receivables find an undue restraint in a system that requires a somewhat lengthy analysis and subsequent written approval by higher authority for an expenditure of only $10,000 in a new piece of equipment.

The system appears artificial and out of proportion to other limitations and controls and is often treated accordingly. The practice in many companies is often reduced to the simple device of beating the system by tailoring the estimates to the point where they will be accepted. Optimistic sales projections are coupled with maximum cost reduction estimates, and the highest attainable rates of production are assumed with the lowest possible allowances for downtime and scrap. This performance is seldom achieved, as the postexpenditure audits show, yet the approach has apparently been useful in getting the authorization approved.

The Need for Integration

This reasoning often gains further support or endorsement from the way in which a manager's performance is evaluated. In many instances, sales and profits alone become the standards of accomplishment and of promotion and financial reward. The related investment or amount of capital required to support the operation may not even be reported or linked with the operating results. This can and does lead managers to regard capital investment as an isolated part of the corporate structure, a part quite separable from the operating factors which receive continuing attention from top management.

These attitudes are often further solidified during the process of annual budgeting in many companies. Here, it is not at all uncommon to have an operating manager submit his annual budget for sales and profit quite independently of any related budget for the investment required and have it approved before any consideration is given to planning for inventories, cash or accounts receivable, or plant and equipment proposals. Although many companies do, in fact, have regular procedures for capital budgeting, very few seem to treat the process as one of integrated financial planning.

Adequate Return as an Objective

The most successful companies in each field have found the long-range value of a somewhat different approach, an approach which fully utilizes the basic role of financial management throughout all aspects of the business functions. They have recognized, for example, that the ultimate goal of operations is neither the management of people nor the management of functions. These have been put into proper perspective as the *means* of coordinating and balancing all corporate activities toward the attainment of the single end objective inherent in any profit-oriented business venture. This objective is *an adequate return on invested capital,* achieved by integrating all the operating and investment plans and decisions around this common focal point.

Once established, the objective provides the starting point from which operating plans and budgets will emanate, and, at the same time, it describes the parameters or probable limits for each area of financial control by defining the interrelationship of every aspect of the business structure. It will, for example, define the profit required to cover the cost of capital employed as well as the combinations of volume and cost that can provide such a profit. Further, it will identify the separate elements of volume, cost, and investment which must be continually adjusted and balanced to meet the changing needs of the business.

To be used in this fashion, the role of financial management must be lifted out of its accounting context and put to work as an operating tool at every level of management. To do this, the nature and the use of invested capital must be defined and understood. The concept of the cost of capital and its relationship to profit objectives must be established, and the interaction of each of the operating objectives must be developed as part of a single unified business plan. From these fundamental objectives, specific operating tools will emerge that will make full use of the concept of financial management itself.

2

The Nature
of Invested Capital

INVESTED capital is, in its simplest terms, nothing more than the money someone has supplied to establish and operate a business. In formal accounting or financial language, it will normally be described in a variety of technical terms as required either by certain contractual obligations or by uniform accounting practice. Typical elements of invested capital found on most balance sheets, for example, will include values ascribed to common stock, preferred stock, capital surplus, and earned surplus or retained earnings. Each of these, including many additional subdivisions concerning different classes of stock and so forth, is merely an identification of the *source* of the capital represented by *ownership* of the business.

Net Worth

In the aggregate, these various accounts are referred to as the *net worth* of the business and represent the amounts of the original funds supplied by the investors or owners of the business plus the accumulated net earnings of the business itself. This latter value, usually described as earned surplus or retained earnings, represents the increase or gain the owners have realized since the start of the business—apart from any dividends or payout of profits they may have received in the meantime.

Although the different classes of stock will share in this pool of capital in varying degrees according to the terms of investment stipulated on their stock certificates, the total of the accounts making up the reported net worth of the company may be thought of as the *equity* capital that the company has available for use. To this extent, the terms "ownership" and "equity" are one and the same thing.

Debt Capital

In addition to the capital furnished by the owners of the business and the accumulated earnings which make up the equity pool, many companies will also raise capital from a second source. This source will consist of *borrowed* funds, monies lent by banks or other lending institutions at varying rates of interest depending on the type of loan and the collateral pledged to secure its repayment. These borrowed funds are also listed on the balance sheet under such typical headings as first mortgage notes, notes payable, bonds, or debentures.

Whether short-term or long-term, all such interest-bearing debt is as much a part of the total invested capital as the stock participation or the capital generated by retained earnings. Thus, where interest-bearing debt is also used, the term *invested capital* will refer to the total of both the equity capital and the debt capital.

Debt and Equity

The link between debt and equity is made more evident when certain features of each are examined and compared.

Preferred stock. For example, preferred stock will be found to have many of the features of a long-term note payable to a bank. It participates in earnings of the company, to be sure, but usually only to the extent of a stipulated preferred dividend which must be met before any additional earnings accrue to the benefit of the common stockholder. In this respect, it can be considered very similar to a note payable that carries a stipulated interest cost which must also be met before earnings or dividends are available for the common equity. Preferred stock will also normally carry a stated value to be paid back in the event of liquidation of the company and, to this extent, is again similar to the face amount due on a note.

Convertible debentures. In addition to these similarities, there is another form of corporate security which is actually a combination of debt and equity in that it includes the elements of both. This is the convertible debenture, a certificate initially issued in the form of a long-term debt with scheduled interest payments, which may, under certain conditions, be con-

verted by the holder into shares of stock and become
part of the equity or ownership of the business.

Debt or Equity as the Source of Capital Funds

There are then two basic forms of invested
capital—debt and equity—which in many instances have
features that are closely linked. They also have one
other very important point in common, in that, in their
several forms, they are simply a description or an identity of the *source* of capital funds. They do not, by themselves, exist in tangible form, nor can they be linked with
any single value such as cash, merchandise, or equipment.

At one point they may have been represented by
cash—cash received from participation in ownership or
in the form of a loan. The cash itself, however, was
immediately commingled into a single fund and was
quickly put to work or *invested* to provide the *assets* required to operate the business. Cash, for example, was
exchanged for buildings and equipment and for raw
materials and supplies, and additional cash was used to
meet payrolls and to pay for operating expenses. The
initial cash, in other words, quickly found its way into
various *asset accounts* such as inventory and equipment
or became tied up in balances due from customers in the
form of accounts receivable from sales.

After a short period of operation, then, the invested
capital has been used to provide the assets of the business and is no longer identifiable in its original form.
This rather simple illustration of the flow of capital
funds into the asset accounts and the subsequent cy-
cling of the assets themselves from cash to labor to in-

ventory to accounts receivable and back again to cash demonstrates one single and fundamental aspect of the nature of invested capital itself. *Capital exists as a common pool of resources and must be managed as a single entity regardless of its original source.* This will become self-evident when the asset accounts are considered at random and a single item in inventory or a single piece of equipment in the plant is taken as an example.

In charting the flow of capital funds from cash into the several asset elements of the business, it will be seen that it is no longer possible to identify the exact source of capital that resulted in the acquisition of any particular asset. One piece of equipment cannot be thought of as having been purchased solely with borrowed funds or another solely from equity capital or from the funds generated by accumulated earnings. Nor is one lot of inventory distinguishable from another as to the *source* of funds used or the order in which the cash was disbursed. Even the amount of capital still residing in the form of cash balances in the bank has become a common pool not directly traceable to its source.

The Use of Capital

The job of raising capital and of deciding how much should be in the form of debt and how much in equity is a highly specialized field that calls for specialized knowledge and expertise, particularly in the more intricate details of the various classes of securities and methods of financing. For this reason, it is far more important for the average manager to know how capital is *used* than it is for him to know how it is raised. If capital is seen as providing the physical assets used in the business, and if the assets themselves are viewed as the tangible values in which the *total* capital has been invested, operating management need not concern itself with the intricacies of stock issues and debt financing.

There is, however, a third source of assets which must be considered before the complexities of accounting classifications and financial statement presentations can be left behind. It has been shown that invested capital supplied in the form of either equity or interest-bearing debt is used to provide assets and that the assets themselves are the tangible values represented by the capital accounts.

Thus, if all labor, materials, supplies, or equipment were paid for immediately in cash, the total of all the asset accounts on the balance sheet would exactly equal the sum of the values represented by the total of all the capital accounts. This would be true because the concept of double-entry bookkeeping would maintain a constant accounted balance between the *source* of the funds (the invested capital) and the *use* of the funds (the asset accounts). Under such conditions, the term "invested capital" would be synonymous with the term "total assets," and the management of capital would become, quite simply, the management of assets themselves.

This situation seldom exists in actual practice, however, since immediate cash payments are neither normal nor desirable in most business operations. As a consequence, the asset accounts will at any given moment in time contain certain items which have been received but not yet paid for and which, therefore, have not been provided by the invested capital of the company. These would include, for example, the materials and supplies received from vendors who will be paid within the next 30 days or possibly the cost of labor that has gone into production and will not be paid for in cash until the following payday. This third source of assets is thus the sum of the values supplied in the short-term by the creditors of the business.

Operating Debt

The assets supplied from this direction are evidenced by the total of the Operating Debt or non-interest-bearing accounts such as the Accounts Payable, Accrued Payroll, Accrued Expenses, and the like. Appearing under the heading of Current Liabilities, the operating debt might be shown as follows in a simplified presentation of a balance sheet:

Assets		*Current Liabilities*	
Cash	$ 100	Accounts Payable	$ 200
Accounts Receivable	200		
Inventories	300	*Invested Capital*	
Plant and		Long-Term Debt	200
Equipment	400	Equity	600
Total	$1,000	Total	$1,000

In such an example, it might be found that the inventory account included purchases of $100 in raw materials which had not yet been paid for and that a new $100 piece of equipment had been added to the plant and equipment assets, with payment due in the following month. The indebtedness for these two items would be represented by the accounts payable liability of $200, leaving the remaining assets financed by the $800 of invested capital. The distinction is important, because the purpose of examining the elements of the asset structure is to *lay a proper foundation for the management of capital*—a task which in turn will lead to a consideration of the cost of capital and its effect on other operating decisions. Since the cost of the assets provided by creditors and others may be assumed to be already included in the prices paid for goods and services, the third source of assets represented by non-interest-bearing debt is excluded from further calculations and is not considered as part of the invested capital base from which profit goals and operating plans will be developed. This is accomplished by a final definition of total invested capital as *the sum of all the assets minus the sum of all of the non-interest-bearing debt.*

This somewhat simplified definition has the further advantage of eliminating in advance the question of whether various reserves and deferred liabilities should be treated as part of invested capital. Such accounts normally appear in a sort of middle ground between the statements of current liabilities and long-term debt and the statements of net worth and are subject to varying interpretations by accountants and financial managers. By considering invested capital to be the net of assets minus operating debt, such accounts are automatically included in the definition of total invested capital, and the result will be found useful for all practical purposes.

How Much Capital Is Needed?

In the long run, the size or level of the total amount of capital employed by a company must conform to its operating needs. If a company continues to grow and expand, it will inevitably need more and more capital to finance its operations. Increased sales will mean a heavier investment in inventories and more funds tied up in accounts receivable from customers. The higher volume will eventually lead to the need for more space and equipment and an increase in working funds to meet expanded payrolls.

As these needs arise, capital may be increased in one of three ways. The first way is from the internal generation of funds realized from profitable operations which are accumulated as earned surplus or retained earnings. Assuming that the company returns only a portion of its current earnings to stockholders in the form of dividends, the accumulation of profits will result in a steady rise in invested capital as long as operations remain profitable. An increase at this rate may be sufficient to meet the needs of a company experiencing a moderate if steady rate of growth, and, under such conditions, no further outside financing would be required.

In other situations, the development of new products or new markets may present opportunities which would be missed if operations were held down to the level permitted by existing capital. In such instances, additional outside capital is raised either by attracting new venture capital in the form of equity investment or by arranging for additional borrowings in the form of interest-bearing debt. In other words, capital is increased either internally or externally, and if it is increased externally it is done by the same process and in essentially the same manner as the original capital was obtained. While these steps may appear fairly obvious, the reverse—the process followed in reducing capital—is not always as readily comprehended or as effectively carried out.

Reducing Capital

In contrast to the company faced with prospects of expanding markets or opportunities for diversification, there are frequent instances of companies whose path remains at a steady level year after year with little prospect for growth but with the ability to maintain an even record of sales and earnings. Whether this results from deliberate corporate policies or from the nature of the particular business or industry, such companies often find themselves faced with an accumulation of capital that greatly exceeds their operating needs.

In such instances, good corporate management dictates a reduction of capital in recognition of the fact that surplus funds might better be invested elsewhere. When such action is taken, it must be recognized that the adjustments must be *external* in the sense that they involve transactions in which capital *flows away* from the company and is returned to the original investors. This might initially take the form of paying off all notes and bonds, thereby eliminating all debt capital. If further reduction should be required, action might next be taken by the company to buy back its own stock or to pay out accumulated earnings in the form of increased dividends. These steps would thus reverse the original process of raising capital and would reduce both the total net assets of the company and the related values carried in the capital accounts.

Reducing investments. The process of reducing capital is often confused with steps taken to reduce *investment* in the various asset accounts themselves. In larger companies where authority and responsibility are decentralized, attention may be focused on the need to speed up the collection of accounts receivable or the need to hold down the investment in the so-called fixed assets of plant and equipment. While these goals may be desirable by themselves, it should be recognized that they do not at this point result in a reduction of the total capital employed.

Each of these actions, if successful, would result merely in moving the investment from one asset account into another. A reduction in inventory, for example, would free up additional cash and thereby increase the cash balance, but it would leave both the total assets and the total capital undisturbed. If such moves were actually aimed at a net reduction in invested capital, the company would then have to follow through by returning capital to the investors.

Managing assets. Since the manager of a single operating unit in the larger company, however, does not ordinarily have authority to reduce the capital of his company—and may not even have access to the ultimate decisions taken in this regard—he must confine his portion of the management of capital to the management of the particular assets under his control. In thus equating a reduction in inventory with a reduction in capital, his actions and those of other managers, taken in the aggregate, actually achieve the same result for the company over a period of time. The immediate result may be to forestall the need for *additional* capital at the corporate level, amounting to a reduction from a projected higher level. Or, if the several individual asset reductions are large enough in the aggregate and can be maintained, the cash thus generated may actually be used to pay off part of the indebtedness or to purchase shares of stock for the company treasury.

Increasing Inventories

Substituting the management of assets at the operating level for the management of capital at the corporate or staff level also has some very practical considerations when proposals are made in the opposite direction—to increase inventories or to add to the investment in plant and machinery. It is not uncommon to hear arguments presented that a proposed investment will cost nothing since "the cash is there anyway." The fallacy in this type of reasoning will become apparent if two investment proposals of equal merit are visualized. The first is accepted on the basis of using idle cash which is assumed to have no capital cost, while the second, and equally good, proposal is rejected since all the idle cash has now been committed and additional capital would thus have to be raised. Investment decisions in a successful business obviously cannot be made on such a "first come, first served" basis, and competent management will take the view that each individual proposal or each increase in assets employed must be considered as as increment of additional capital. This can have a profound effect on evaluating a series of investment proposals, particularly when each is subjected to an analysis that recognizes the true cost of capital employed.

3

The Cost of Capital

THE cost of capital employed in a business venture is perhaps the keystone of financial management itself, since it will in turn determine the amount of capital used and will govern all subsequent actions and operating decisions aimed at the generation of profits.

Capital has a cost, and the cost of capital must be recovered in the same sense that the cost of materials or the cost of labor and overhead must be recovered before any final profit can be said to exist. In the same fashion that the costs of materials and supplies are established in the marketplace by the supplier and the costs of salaries and wages are established by the worker through negotiation or contract demands, the cost of capital is established by the investor. While not as evident or as directly measurable as the costs of labor and materials, it nonetheless exists and must be taken into account.

Cost of Capital Determined by the Investor

The cost of capital to a company is the composite rate of return demanded by the investor. The company may negotiate for the use of capital as it negotiated for the costs of materials and labor, seeking to secure the best terms available in open competition with others, but the eventual price to be paid will be determined in each case by the supplier.

The supplier of goods and services will calculate his price on the basis of cost, the volume to be produced, and the related investment required to support or finance the entire transaction. The supplier of capital is not offering goods or services for which a price must be paid; he is offering money which he wants to put to work. His cost will be determined not by estimates of work performed or materials consumed, *but by the risk to which he puts the money he is willing to invest.*

The investor's assessment of risk is not readily discernible in his step-by-step evaluation of the enterprise. He will, for example, appraise the nature of the business and its position within its industry, the past record of accomplishment if any, and the type and amount of capital to be used; he then will attempt to evaluate the quality and the capability of management in arriving at his composite appraisal of risk.

In making his appraisal, the investor will also have considered the various other choices or opportunities open to him for the investment of capital and will weigh the *relative risks* involved in such alternatives in establishing his price for capital. Since the price he will demand will, in the aggregate, become the cost of capital to the company, *the rate of return to the investor will become the rate of cost or the rate of return on capital* required by the company.

Exhibit 1

*Relationship of Risk and Cost of Capital ***

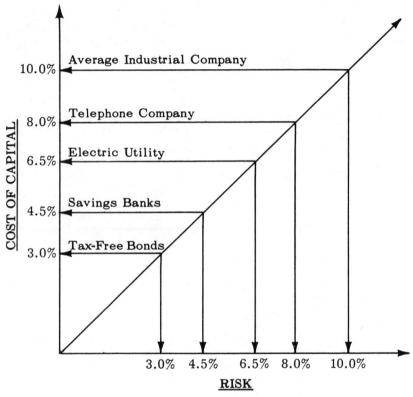

* Assuming a constant 6% prime rate for money.

The appraisal of risk which leads to the determination of the cost of capital may be seen more readily if viewed through the eyes of the investor in the process of evaluating the various opportunities for investment and the degree of risk that each will entail. His approach to this selection might, for example, progress through the series of steps shown in Exhibit 1 as he weighs the advantages, the opportunities, and the limitations of several alternatives.

Investment Alternatives

Taken in the order of increasing risk, his first choice is to do nothing. Assuming that the funds were simply placed in a strongbox and locked safely away, and ignoring any future erosion of the purchasing power of the funds, his risk would be at point zero. Because the risk would be zero, it is obvious that the rate of return would also be zero, since the two have a direct relationship.

If instead the funds were invested in, say, tax-free municipal bonds, the investor might reasonably expect a return of around 3 percent on his investment since the risk, in the aggregate, is considered by investors as a group to be 3 percent. While municipal bonds are generally backed up or guaranteed by the taxing authority of the municipality, some issues may occasionally be defaulted or may fail to meet their scheduled interest payments and hence have a composite risk when considered as a group. At a return of 3 percent to the investor, the assessment of risk has also established a 3 percent cost to the borrower.

In seeking a higher rate of return on his money, the investor might next turn to the idea of savings deposits which might earn an average of some 4.5 percent on the funds invested. Again, the rate of return to the investor would represent an average cost of capital of 4.5 percent to the savings institutions, since the risk is also considered to be 4.5 percent for this form of investment. The composite risk in savings accounts will be seen more readily when sums in excess of the limits of coverage offered by the Federal Deposit Insurance Corporation are involved and when investment is broadly defined as including all forms of banks, credit unions, and savings and loan institutions.

At this point the investor would recognize that, while he had limited his *risk* in investing in either municipal bonds or savings accounts, he had also completely limited his *opportunity* for possible gain by accepting a fixed-obligation security in exchange for safety of principal. Not content with this, he might logically seek out greater opportunities for profit for which he would then be willing to take on a higher risk.

The next most logical choices might then be in the form of equity investment in shares of an electric utility company or in shares of telephone stock. Since the return on invested capital in each is regulated by public authority, the investor could expect a return in the range of 6 percent to 8 percent for this type of investment. The average rate of return in electric utilities, for example, might be found at around 6.5 percent, since the risk is considered somewhat lower than an investment in telephone stock at 7.5 percent to 8 percent. In this area, the regulatory authority of the government has, in fact, given recognition to the investors' appraisal of risk by defining and limiting ahead of time the permissible rate of return on invested capital that a public utility may earn to cover its cost of capital. In so doing, it gives recognition to the cost of obtaining capital, the rates of return of other companies, and the risks the utility has either assumed or may become exposed to.

When the judgments of the regulatory bodies fail to coincide with the aggregate investor appraisal of risk, and the allowed rate of return on capital is artificially lowered, for example, the investor will invariably turn away to more lucrative opportunities. More specifically, when the risk and hence the cost of capital remains at 8 percent in the opinion of the investor, a reduction to 7 percent in the allowed rate of return on capital for a public utility will succeed only in drying up the market for available capital. Recognition of such investor reaction and the workings of the basic economic forces which motivate investor decisions has led the regulatory authority on occasion to reconsider its rulings and to adjust the required parity between risk and the return on invested capital.

These alternative investment opportunities—ranging from municipal bo.ids at 3 percent to telephone stocks at 8 percent—merely form the foundation or perhaps the background for arriving at the cost of capital for the average industrial company, which is not regulated by public authority but operates competitively in a free-enterprise system. Without restrictions or regulations on its earning power, it is also without a prescribed or clearly defined cost of capital. How, then, is the cost of capital for the industrial enterprise established? Who determines the rate of return required, and how can it be measured?

Cost—A Subjective Figure

For those who demand absolute proof in the form of facts and figures or who seek a quick calculation from some mathematical equation or formula, going beyond this point will prove difficult. For the truth is that the cost of capital for industry cannot be determined with any degree of exactitude in the short term, it cannot be counted or weighed or measured in precise numbers, and it cannot be demonstrated or found in the casting up of corporate accounts.

The cost of capital is, by its nature, imprecise and somewhat subjective in interpretation and projection. It is also, for these reasons, often misunderstood or neglected completely in the field of business management. It can, however, be ascertained within reasonable limits, both by the process of inductive reasoning and by a review of historical relationships between corporate earnings and the rate at which such earnings have been capitalized by the investor.

In approaching a solution by inductive reasoning, the foregoing examples of alternative investment opportunities serve to establish a probable minimum for the cost of capital in the average industrial company. If such sheltered investments as bonds, savings accounts, and shares of regulated utilities can offer as much as an 8 percent return on capital for correspondingly low risks, it would not appear likely that an obviously higher risk in the commercial and industrial fields would fall below the 8 percent level. With this as a base, it would then be reasonable to extrapolate a cost-of-capital range somewhere between 8 percent and infinity.

Ruling out the extreme situations of pure speculation or the magnitude of risk inherent in a throw of dice or a game of chance, certain practical limitations are also indicated at the top side of the range, well short of the theoretical assumption of infinity. Dealing only with what might be considered normal business ventures, the upper limit might be described as around 25 percent, for all practical purposes. Moreover, this limit would be confined to the forefront of new technology and ideas where no historical data exist as a guide to probable results and the future of the enterprise is indeed a high-risk situation.

From such an analysis, it is possible to define a *probable* range of 8 percent to 25 percent as the cost of capital for the average industrial company. When compared with the more precise figures for other investments, such a range is obviously too broad to be useful or to provide a measurable cost of capital for the average company. Further tests must be applied if a working tool is to be developed.

Average Cost of Capital *

Exhibit 1 sets an average cost for industrial capital at 10 percent, placing it above the 8 percent base but well below the indicated upper limits that have been assumed. This suggests, first, that the *average* of all industrial companies is only slightly higher than the average for the regulated utilities and, second, that some evidence exists to support the assumption of a 10 percent average cost of capital. Such evidence does exist, but again it is tenuous and serves only as a check on the reasonableness or probability of the assumptions previously arrived at. The evidence is found in two areas, the first factual and the second analytical or interpretive.

The average earnings of a broad segment of industrial companies have consistently averaged a 10 percent return on invested capital over a period of years, and stock market prices over an equal period have reflected a direct relationship to the earnings on invested capital. While these figures by no means establish any form of proof, they at least tend to support the probability of the assumptions and perhaps to indicate a working range within which the cost of capital might be defined more exactly. To do this, two extremes in the capital structure of a single company might be considered.

* Again, assuming a constant 6.0% prime rate for money.

Capital as Debt

If all capital were in the form of debt, the cost of capital would be readily determinable and easily understood. Debt is paid for in the form of interest, and, since interest rates are established ahead of time, the total interest charges applied to the total amount of debt employed would give an exact and absolute measure of the cost of capital. If such financing were possible, the several individual interest rates involved would also be a direct measure of the risk assumed by the lender. The first layer of debt, for example—the senior debt—might be secured by first-mortgage notes for which the land and buildings of the firm had been pledged as collateral. Since the risk to the lender would be relatively low, such debt might carry an interest rate of 6 percent.

The next layer of debt might be found in bonds which had pledged certain other assets of the company or perhaps restricted the use of cash in an attempt to conserve the operating capital of the organization. The bonds, having less security than the mortgage notes, might carry an interest rate of 7 percent.

For the third layer of debt, the company might issue debentures, promissory notes issued against the general credit of the corporation for which no collateral would be available. Since the risk at this point would now be considerably higher, the company might have to pay as high as 9 percent in interest charges. In raising the remaining capital—all in the form of debt—the company would then have to turn to less reliable sources of capital and pay the price for speculative funds. In such a case, if a source could indeed be found, the interest rates on the last layer of debt might easily be 20 percent or 25 percent for relatively short-term money.

Taken in the aggregate, the total interest charges would equal at least 10 percent on the total borrowed capital and could be figured exactly and measured as a precise quantity. In other words, if the earnings of the business were exactly equal to the interest charges on borrowed money, the cost of capital would be paid and management would have an exact measure of performance.

Such a capital structure is, however, confined to the realm of theory. From a purely legal point of view, a corporation cannot exist without some form of *ownership,* so that a small amount of equity would have to be present to make such a structure even remotely possible. On the more practical side, a substantial amount of equity would have to exist first before the corporation could be considered to have any borrowing power. The use of debt is therefore limited by economic considerations, if nothing else, and will be found to be a relatively minor part of the total capital employed in most companies, averaging perhaps 30% of the total capital. The relationship is often referred to in financial reports as the debt/equity ratio, and is useful as a measure of the extent to which a company has used its borrowing capacity.

Capital as Equity

The other extreme in capital structure would be found in the company that had no debt and had a capital investment consisting entirely of ownership or equity capital. In this case, there would be no interest charges on which to base the cost of capital and hence no related costs would appear in the operating statements. The stock certificates would not stipulate any required rate of return to the stockholders, and, in fact, no fixed obligation of any kind would exist that required any earnings or any return to the investors.

Dividends are not comparable to interest charges since management, not the investor, will set the dividend rate and may on occasion decide to omit the dividend entirely. Not even the dividends on preferred stock, which normally must be paid before any dividend is available for the common stockholder, would qualify as a partial measure of the cost of capital. Preferred dividends are simply the right of the preferred stockholder to receive his share first—if indeed there is anything to share. In brief, the cost of equity capital is *not* specified in any manner similar to the interest cost on borrowed money. Is there, then, an actual cost for equity capital? And if there is, how is it measured?

The answers to these questions will again be found in the evaluation of risk, an evaluation made by a single investor or by investors as a group over a period of time. Since the investor has been asked to put his money out at risk, he will demand a return on his investment commensurate with the same degree of risk. He will quantify his evaluation of risk, in effect, by naming the price he is willing to pay for a share of stock. If his assessment of the several factors of management competence, type of business and industry position, size of the capital employed, and potential earning power is high, he will have considered the venture as a relatively low risk and pay a relatively high price for a share of the equity.

If, on the other hand, the investor has a somewhat lower opinion of the company's overall capability or if the earnings record of the company in recent years has been less than satisfactory, he will assign a higher risk factor and pay less for his participation. In either case, the investor is determining the cost of capital for the company by naming the *price* he is willing to pay for the stock. Disregarding the brokerage fees or underwriting costs which the company must also bear for a new stock issue—and which will add some 15 percent to the cost of raising equity capital—*the fundamental cost to the company will be the earnings requirement that the equity investor has placed on it.*

Price/Earnings Ratio

The investor's appraisal of risk is thus translated into the price he is willing to pay for a share of stock. The price, in turn, is based on an expectation of earnings— earnings which will accrue to him as the owner of the business and which will compensate or reward him for the risk he has taken. The earnings may be returned to him in part in the form of dividends, but in the main they will be reflected in the increased value of his participation as evidenced by the retained earnings or earned surplus of the company. In turn, the earnings retained in the business provide additional capital which can be put to work so that, if the business prospers, his share will be increased at a compound rate.

Since the price the investor will pay is thus based on the earning power of the company, the relationship is usually measured in terms of the *price/earnings ratio,* which is simply another way of measuring the cost of equity capital in terms of the earnings required. If the overall assessment of risk is low, the investor will pay more for earnings and the cost of capital to the company will be reduced. If the risk is considered high, the earnings will command a lower price and the cost of capital will thus increase correspondingly. If, for example, a company reports earnings of $1 a share on its stock and the stock is quoted at $5 a share, the price/earnings ratio is expressed as 5:1. From the investor's point of view, the overall risk is high and he is willing to pay only five times earnings, which will yield a 20 percent return on his investment. From the company point of view, the cost of equity capital is now 20 percent since the company must provide $1 in earnings to attract $5 in capital. If at a later point in time the stock were to sell at $10 a share on reported earnings of $1, the price/earnings ratio would have risen to 10:1, and the company would have a 10 percent cost of capital since the $1 in earnings would now attract $10 in capital investment.

Market Quotations—
An Inadequate Yardstick

An analysis of this sort would lead to the natural assumption that a company's cost of capital could be measured directly from current market quotations and was subject to constant change as the market fluctuated from day to day. If this were true, it would also then follow that the more volatile issues selling at 50 times earnings had a basic cost of only 2 percent for equity capital—a rate well below the rate of interest for savings deposits. Neither assumption is accurate, although the implied relationship of market price to the cost of capital will remain valid if put in the proper perspective.

Short-term changes do not show basic values. The cost of capital cannot be measured directly from current market quotations for several reasons. To begin with, the market itself is subject to short-term adjustments, either up or down, which often bear little resemblance to basic values. The term "investor" actually represents the entire investing public, a population which ranges from the professional money-managers to the doctors, lawyers, businessmen, schoolteachers, housewives, and the like, who may buy or sell only a few shares at a time, but who as a group account for a large percentage of the total funds invested. The former group is generally sophisticated in its approach and relies on fundamental values in its decision making. The latter group is often motivated by tips or rumors and frequently deals more with emotion than with logic.

The cumulative effect of the decisions these people make to buy or sell a certain security at a given price can have a substantial influence on the short-term fluctuation of quoted prices. In the longer term, the market will eventually adjust to prices which more nearly reflect the earning power of a security and which correlate more directly with the cost-of-capital concept. Even here, the task of analysis and interpretation is not a simple one since the long-term average for market performance may easily mean a period of ten years or more.

New capital is not raised continuously. Companies do not raise new capital every day of the week, every month, or even every year. The cost of capital will thus be found only at periodic intervals when companies actually find it necessary to go to the marketplace for new capital and to meet the investors' demands for a rate of return. While interim price quotations may serve as a general guide to the probable price/earnings ratio for a new stock issue, the cost of capital can be seen only as a concept until the time comes to demonstrate its existence by raising new capital. This fact, however, makes it doubly important that the concept itself be properly understood and that it be fully used in the day-to-day financial management of the business, since its success or failure will eventually determine the future cost of doing business. This will be true even of the company that has no foreseeable need for additional capital at any point during its corporate existence.

Loss of capital. The same forces which serve to attract new capital can cause capital to *flow away* from a business. If the cost-of-capital concept is ignored and the operating margins of a company over a period of time are insufficient to justify the use and the risk of the capital employed, capital will begin to flow into more profitable channels. The loss of capital might first appear in the inability to renew various segments of the debt capital as it approached maturity or the inability to refund because of sharply increased demands for higher interest rates. Finally, the equity capital itself could be subject to dissolution by action of the stockholders in demanding higher dividends or the termination of certain branch or product-line operations with a subsequent return of capital from the proceeds.

In summary, perhaps only the family-owned business would appear to be immune to the consequences of a failure to earn the cost of capital. Since the manager and the investor are one and the same, it might be argued that the concept could not apply or had no practical implications. This would be true if the individual owner-manager were content to "idle" his investment or to realize less return on his own capital than it would bring elsewhere. Because few people are inclined in this direction, however, the concept remains valid and is usually put into practice.

Investor expectations. Finally, current market quotations cannot be assumed to reflect the current cost of capital for a very fundamental reason having to do with *investor expectations.* The investor who pays 50 times the current per-share earnings of a company is not assessing the prospects at a 2 percent risk, nor is he content with a 2 percent return on his investment—a return which would indicate no more than a 2 percent cost of capital for the company. He is, however, willing to pay a premium on the basis of present earnings for the prospect of substantially increased *future earnings,* and in doing so he is said to be "discounting" the earnings growth.

If, for example, a company had established a consistent record of rapid growth in reaching a present level of $1 per-share earnings, an investor might be willing to pay $50 a share or 50 times earnings in the expectation that two things would happen: First, the earnings would continue to increase rapidly to the point where his initial investment would soon represent 10 times earnings or less, giving him an *average* price/earnings multiple at least commensurate with the risk; and second, other investors would view the trend the same way and would continue to pay a premium for current earnings at any future point at which he might choose to sell. The higher the ratio to current earnings, the greater is the expectation of a capital gain by a sale to the next buyer, since the expectation of future earnings may not be realized for many years.

Prices Eventually Seek Normal Levels

In spite of the short-term fluctuation in the market price of corporate equity and the obviously speculative nature of the abnormally high price/earnings ratios to be found in certain stock issues, experience has shown that, over a long enough period of time, prices will seek a "normal" level in relation to earnings. It is this basic or normal level which more accurately reflects the long-range appraisal of risk and which, in turn, establishes the cost of capital.

Historically, this level has been placed at ten times earnings for the average industrial/commercial company, and the resulting 10 percent cost of capital has served as a useful rule of thumb when related to an assumed constant 6.0% prime rate for money.

With an approximate average thus established for industry as a whole, further steps can be taken to identify more closely the cost of capital for a single industry within a group or for a single company within a particular industry. As with any average number, the average cost of capital will include some risks below the 10 percent level and some well above it. These can be categorized by analysis of earnings trends in relation to the average market price of securities over a period of time. Then the categories can be narrowed down to a useful working range by a more detailed study of published reports for the leading companies within each industry group. The ability to develop an exact calculation, however, is far less important than the use of the concept itself. Once the cost of capital has been recognized as a basic element of the cost of operations, a derived order-of-magnitude figure may well suffice for the purposes of financial planning and control.

Cost of Capital Not Related
to the Source of Funds

Thus far, the relationship of risk to cost of capital employed has been examined separately for a theoretical all-debt capital structure and for an all-equity or debt-free company. The examples given might easily lead to the assumption that capital has in fact *two* costs—one for debt and one for equity—and that the composite cost to a company would therefore depend on the *source* of the capital rather than on the use to which it was put. Such is not the case.

The risk of the enterprise itself will determine the rate of return required by the investor and will thus establish the cost of capital to the company. *It is the use to which capital is put* that will determine its cost and not the source of capital itself. In other words, capital has a cost as an entity by itself based on the total risk of the enterprise, regardless of whether that capital is supplied in the form of debt or in the form of equity. As has been seen, capital is used to provide assets, and, once used, its source is no longer identifiable. In the form of assets, capital constitutes a common pool and thus has a common cost. This point is not always recognized in planning for the use of capital.

If a business is assumed to be a 10 percent risk and can finance a portion of its capital requirements through debt capital at an interest cost of only 6 percent, it might appear that the overall cost of capital had been reduced below 10 percent—that, in fact, debt could be used to minimize both the risk and the cost. This would be true if the cost of equity capital remained a constant, but in practice it does not.

The underlying concept that will govern the total

cost of total capital is that *the cost of equity capital will eventually increase in direct proportion to the amount and type of debt employed.* The use of debt financing carries with it a prior claim to certain assets of the business and often certain restrictions on the use of operating funds. The introduction of debt into the capital structure will therefore increase the risk of the equity shareholder, and his assessment of that increased risk will result in a higher cost for the equity portion of capital. For this reason, every investment decision made by a company must consider the *total* cost of capital employed, and the projected return on the proposed investment must be sufficient to recover that cost.

Actions which run contrary to the principle of a total cost for total capital will result in an eventual loss of capital. For example, a company may be considering a major increase in the funds invested in inventory as part of a marketing program to increase the volume of sales. The calculations of incremental profit may show a pretax return of 7 percent on the added investment in inventory, and the company is in a position where it can borrow the necessary funds on a long-term note at 6 percent interest. The attitude of many operating managers in such a case is that the move would be profitable because the added profit would more than cover the interest cost and would, in fact, leave a 1 percent gain in operating profits. The point which is not understood in this reasoning process is that the additional funds would be employed at a pretax 20 percent risk and that a projected 7 percent return would yield, not a profit, but a 13 percent loss of capital.

The penalties of such decisions, however, are not immediate. The effect is a cumulative one that, over a period of many years, gradually weakens the fabric of the corporate structure and builds up a delayed cost which must eventually be paid. Because management is often motivated more by the promise of immediate rewards or by the effects of an immediate penalty, the cost of capital is often regarded as an abstract subject, not directly measurable and therefore largely theoretical. With this approach, many short-term decisions are made which may increase the total dollars of profit reported, but which ignore the amount of capital required to earn these same profits. The result is a steady erosion of earning power, reflected in a decreasing rate of return on invested capital.

Successful Capital Management

To be successful, a company must evaluate the cost of the capital it employs and then give recognition to that cost in the setting of goals and objectives and in the execution of these objectives in the processes of planning, operating, controlling, and evaluating. Management, for its part, must accept a stewardship for the capital funds entrusted to its care and must fulfill its obligation to put such capital to work at a true profit to the investor.

4

The Measurement
of Return on Capital

THE cost of capital has been described as the starting
point for financial management because of its fundamental role in planning and controlling profits. In setting profit goals for a company or in evaluating the results of operations, profits cannot properly be measured
in terms of dollar amounts or as a percentage of sales
income. Not until profits are measured in relation to the
amount of capital required to earn them do they take on
any valid meaning or provide any measurable level of
accomplishment. Although other measures have a
proper place and a proper use in *balancing* the results of
the individual elements of the business structure, the
final appraisal can be made only when profits are expressed as a percentage return on invested capital.

What Is Return on Invested Capital?

Since such a measure must also become the focal point for all financial planning and decision making, it is necessary for management to have a clear understanding of how the measurement is made, what it is based on, and, in particular, what it means when compared with the other ratios and other measurements which are frequently applied to earnings. Return on invested capital does not, for example, have the same meaning or the same value as return on assets and can differ widely from such customary yardsticks as return on equity and earnings per share.

Taken in its simplest form in order to establish the relationship of profit to capital, it would be necessary only to determine the net earnings for the period and the amount of invested capital and to divide the earnings by the capital to determine the rate of return. In condensed form, the figures might appear as follows:

Sales	$2,000	Common Stock	$ 400
Operating Costs	1,800	Retained Earnings	600
Pretax Profit	200	Invested Capital	$1,000
Taxes @ 50%	100		
Net Earnings	$ 100		

$$\frac{\text{Net Earnings } \$100}{\text{Invested Capital } \$1,000} = 10\% \text{ Return on invested capital}$$

The Element of Debt Capital

In such a simplified example, the return on equity would also be 10 percent since all the invested capital exists in the form of equity. If, however, the capital structure were changed to include the use of debt capital, two changes would appear in the analysis and in the interpretation of the results. First, the return on equity would no longer equal the overall return on invested capital, since the total capital would now include the use of debt which in turn had helped to create the total net earnings. The return on equity would assume, on the other hand, that all net earnings over and above the interest cost of the debt itself were attributable to the equity capital and would measure the entire net earnings reported as a percentage return on only the equity portion of the invested capital. Second, the use of debt would introduce an anomaly into the reported operating results of net earnings after taxes. The accounting presentation of the operating statement would include all costs and related expenses matched against the income for the period in arriving at the reported book earnings, *including the interest charges on the debt portion of the capital employed.*

In other words, the earnings report would already have taken into account part of the cost of capital—the interest on the debt capital—but would have made no similar provision for the remaining cost of capital represented by the equity investment. The only available means of determining whether the cost of capital had been recovered is by measuring the net return on capital employed against the assumed cost of the capital. It would thus be necessary to make some adjustment in the analysis of the figures to avoid a double charge for the cost of the debt capital. Where debt is used as a part of the permanent capital of the business, therefore, the interest charges on the debt must be added back to the accounted earnings. This will give the effect of presenting a picture of *total earnings on total capital* and will preserve the meaning of the resulting rate of return.

The Impact of the Use of Debt

Adjusting the previous example to include the use of debt would expand the analysis and alter the meaning of some of the values:

Sales	$2,000	Debt @ 6%	$ 200
Operating Costs	1,800	Common Stock	200
Operating Margin	200	Retained Earnings	600
Interest Cost	12	Invested Capital	$1,000
Pretax Profit	188		
Taxes @ 50%	94		
Net Earnings	$ 94		

Reported Book Earnings	$ 94
Add After-Tax Interest Cost	6
Total Earnings on Capital	$100

$$\frac{\text{Total Earnings } \$100}{\text{Invested Capital } \$1,000} = 10\% \text{ Return on invested capital}$$

In comparison with the first example, the reported net earnings have dropped to $94 since the interest cost on the debt portion of the capital has been charged against current operations. The return on invested capital, however, has remained unchanged at 10 percent since there has been no change in actual total earnings from operations or in the total amount of capital employed. The return on equity, on the other hand, would now measure the reported book earnings of

$94 against the $800 of equity investment and report an improved rate of return amounting to 11.75 percent:

	Debt	Equity	Total Capital	Book Earn-ings	Percent Return on Capital	Percent Return on Equity
Case I	—	$1,000	$1,000	$100	10.0	10.0
Case II	$200	800	1,000	94	10.0	11.75

In comparing these figures it will be noted that, while the return on invested capital has remained constant at 10 percent, the reported return on equity has shown a 1.75 percent increase. Which is right? Which more accurately reflects the results of operations and the use of capital?

The "Leverage" Theory

In the sense that they are mathematically correct, both measurements are right. But, in the sense that they represent trends or improved operating results, the reports for return on equity can be highly misleading. One school of thought which subscribes to the leverage theory of financial management would claim that the use of debt capital was beneficial to the stockholder and would point to the higher return on equity as evidence of the gain which had accrued to the equity through the use of debt. Such reasoning would stem from the position that, if money could be borrowed at 6 percent and put to work at 10 percent, the added earnings of 4 percent over and above the cost of interest on the borrowed money accrued to the equity participation, thereby in-

creasing the leverage on earnings. Although it is true
that all earnings above the cost of interest do, in fact,
belong to the equity shareholder, the shareholder has
not, in the examples cited, actually received any gain or
improvement whatsoever in the reported jump from 10
percent to 11.75 percent in return on equity. What is
missing from the analysis is the degree by which the risk
to the common equity has been increased by adding
debt to the capital structure. In this example, at least,
the risk can be considered to have increased in direct
proportion to the rate of return on equity, since operating income has remained unchanged as has the total
amount of capital employed. In other words, the rate of
return *should have increased* to 11.75 percent just to hold
the profit position in relation to the risk of capital. The
fact that it did is verified by the measurement of return
on invested capital, which showed no change from the
10 percent previously reported. In short, return on
equity is completely valid only when no debt financing is
used or when debt itself remains at a constant level in
the capital structure. Return on total capital, on the
other hand, is not dependent on changes in the source
of capital and can be used as a constant measure of
overall financial performance.

Return on Assets

Neither return on equity nor return on total capital
is normally synonymous with a third measure which
finds frequent use in financial reports—the return on
assets. Because total assets are normally larger than the
total capital employed, owing to the level of assets furnished by trade creditors, the rate of return on assets

will be somewhat lower than the corresponding rate of return on capital. While by no means as misleading as the figures for return on equity, the percentages reported for return on assets can prove erratic at times because the calculation ignores the management of operating debt.

Invested capital has been defined for all practical purposes as the sum of the total assets minus the sum of the operating debt. Thus, if a company can manage a larger share of its total assets by taking full advantage of the payment terms to creditors, it can utilize larger assets with no corresponding increase in invested capital. The measurement of return on capital will recognize this factor and will reflect a higher rate of return when trade payables are increased. The calculations for return on assets will not, but will measure the net earnings against the *total* assets employed, whether those assets have been provided by the invested capital of the business or by the level of assets furnished by trade creditors. Of the two, the return on invested capital is again the more useful measure since it takes all the operating elements of the business into account.

Earnings per Share

The fourth and by far the most commonly used measurement of earnings is that of earnings per share. This simply divides the reported dollars of net earnings by the number of shares outstanding and reports earnings in terms of so many dollars and cents per share of stock. In the two examples that were used earlier, the reports of earnings per share might be determined as follows:

	Book Earnings	*Number of Shares*	*Earnings per Share*
Case I	$100	400	$.25
Case II	94	200	.47

Here, the substitution of $200 of debt for $200 of common stock has had a pronounced effect on the earnings measurement used, showing a reported gain or an increase of nearly 100 percent in what is often interpreted as the earning power of the company. In reality, nothing has changed; the total return on invested capital is 10 percent in both cases. As reported on the basis of earnings per share, however, the total book earnings of the company have simply been divided by half the previous number of shares. The result is a doubling of the earnings per share, a figure which is then reduced slightly by the effect of interest charges taken against current income.

Of all the earnings measurements used, the report of earnings per share is perhaps the poorest in that it ignores the total amount of capital employed and can frequently present a picture of earnings which is exactly the opposite of the financial performance of the company as a whole. Even where no debt is used, the gradual increase in retained earnings resulting from profitable operations will increase the total equity investment, so that a corresponding increase in the *dollars of profit* will be needed just to maintain a constant rate of return on capital. If the dollars of profit should increase at a slower rate than the growth of capital, the return on invested capital will gradually decrease—while, with a constant number of shares of stock outstanding, the earnings per share will show a consistent gain! This can be illustrated by the example of a company whose initial capital is represented by 100 shares of common stock originally issued at $10 a share, whose earnings start in the first year at $100 and increase at the rate of approximately 5 percent a year, and whose earnings have been plowed back into the company for further growth instead of being paid out as dividends.

Year	Earn- ings	Invested Capital	Earn- ings per Share	Percent Return on Capital
1	$100	$1,000	$1.00	10.0
2	105	1,100	1.05	9.5
3	110	1,205	1.10	9.1
4	115	1,315	1.15	8.7
5	120	1,430	1.20	8.4

The missing element. In this example, the use of the earnings-per-share measurement as perhaps the sole criterion of financial success has given the investor the picture of a solid 20 percent increase in earnings, when, in fact, the true profit performance of the company has fallen off some 16 percent when measured in terms of total capital employed. The missing element is, of course, *the measure of how much earnings should have increased* as more and more capital was put to work.

Management confusion. It is not only the investor who may be confused or misled by such reports. Management itself, using earnings per share as its basic financial objective, will often follow a course of action aimed solely at increasing the per-share results, even though such actions may well reduce the total return on total capital invested. When motivated in this direction, management would, for example, be reluctant to shut down a marginal operation which had no probability of recovering its own cost of capital. Even though the phasing-

out of the low-income-producing facility and the subsequent liquidation of its supporting capital investment
would markedly improve the overall financial results of
the company, the fact that *some* earnings were being
generated and were therefore contributing to the
earnings-per-share report would act as a deterrent to a
logical decision or program for corrective action.

Such situations are, unfortunately, not uncommon
even though a very brief analysis of the financial elements involved will often disclose the price a company is
paying for its per-share record. Management will frequently put such emphasis on per-share earnings in its
reports to stockholders that it will set targets for per-
share results that are soon regarded as the prime objective of being in business.

An example of a company faced with a major decision in one of its product-line operations will serve to
illustrate the point. The product line in question has
shown a particularly poor record of earnings for several
years in a row, projections of future earnings show no
probability of improvement, and the product is not
needed to support the sales of other lines in the company. Proposals to shut down the operation, however,
have brought up the question of the effect on earnings
per share for the current year. The company has reported a steady growth in per-share results in the past
and has committed itself to a target of 70 cents a share
for the current period. It faces the following situation:

	Capital	Earnings	Earnings per Share	Percent Return on Capital
Product line A	$ 4,000	$ 40	$.04	1
All other lines	6,000	660	.66	11
Total company	$10,000	$700	$.70	7

From such an analysis, it is obvious that complete liquidation of the marginal operation would result in a substantial improvement in overall return on invested capital and that such a move would clearly be in the best interests of the investors. The reluctance to forgo the additional 4 cents a share in its reported earnings, however, may easily defer or even completely block the necessary action.

Such instances are by no means limited to situations involving the elimination of marginal activities. The same approach is often found in considering proposals for *new* ventures, whether they be new product lines, expanded branch operations, or even the acquisition of other companies. Since this type of operating philosophy does work with equal force in both directions, it suggests the strong need for a better and more concrete form of financial appraisal.

The Basic Purpose of Management

In the long run, management must look to the overall return on invested capital—if for no other reason than the fact that the investor himself will sooner or later appraise the operating results on this basis. Since the business is being run for the investor, he will ultimately dictate a change in management if his funds are not employed profitably. Good operating management will therefore evaluate its cost of capital and establish a set of objectives and profit goals which will dictate a specified rate of return on capital as the basic purpose of being in business. To implement such objectives, it will need to develop working tools which will establish operating standards for each element of the business, so that the interaction of business decisions can be adjusted or continually brought into balance in order to achieve the overall desired results. The development of such working tools, in turn, will require a closer examination of the relationship of capital to volume, volume to profit, and profit to capital.

The Use of "Average" Capital Employed

The measurement of return on capital has been shown as the process of dividing the earnings by the capital, with the result expressed in terms of a percentage return on capital employed. It has also been shown that the reported book earnings do not always represent a true statement of results, since interest charges must be added in order to determine *total* earnings where debt is involved. With earnings thus properly adjusted, they should then be measured against the invested capital which was used to provide the earnings. This will not be simply the capital balance at the beginning of the fiscal period, nor will it be the comparable balance at the end. Since income was produced *during* the period, a proper measurement requires the calculation of *average* capital employed during the same period of time.

Capital investment can, and frequently does, change substantially from time to time as earnings are plowed back into the business, new equity capital is raised, or debt financing is added or deleted from the capital structure. For all practical purposes, a reasonable statement of average capital employed can be developed in most business situations by simply taking a series of monthly averages of the beginning and ending capital balances.

Even with the earnings and invested capital figures thus adjusted, the use of the computed rate of return on average capital would appear to fall short of the requirements needed to make it a useful tool for current operating decisions. The mere mathematics of the calculation would seem to suggest that it can be computed only after the fact or at the end of the operating period, that the factors must be developed from such isolated reports as the profit and loss statement and the balance sheet, and that these sources do not offer a practical means of guiding the multitude of decisions which must be made on a day-to-day basis throughout all levels of management.

Turnover of Capital

The measurement of return on capital can, however, be translated into terms which will measure the two primary elements which control the rate of return itself and which will, in turn, provide the working tools needed for planning and controlling as well as for evaluating the effects of current operating decisions. The measurement of these two primary elements can be illustrated by using the same figures shown in the original example, which described the overall return on capital calculation:

Sales	$2,000
Earnings	100
Capital	1,000

The formula to determine the rate of return on capital was given as

$$\frac{\text{Earnings (\$100)}}{\text{Capital (\$1,000)}} = \text{Rate of return (10\%)}$$

If, instead, the volume of sales income is first related to the average invested capital, a factor for the turnover of capital can be established:

$$\frac{\text{Sales (\$2,000)}}{\text{Capital (\$1,000)}} = \text{Turnover (2)}$$

This factor measures the rate at which the dollars of capital are turned in relation to the dollars of sales—the turnover of invested capital. Expressed another way, the company has been able to generate $2 of sales for every $1 of capital invested. This relationship will later become one of the key financial measurements in evaluating proposals for added investment in assets employed and in balancing the need for added investment against the projected incremental dollars of sales.

Percentage of Net Earnings to Sales

The second primary element to be measured is the relationship of earnings to the dollar volume of sales, which establishes a factor for *the percentage of net earnings to sales:*

$$\frac{\text{Earnings (\$100)}}{\text{Sales (\$2,000)}} = \text{Earnings to sales (5\%)}$$

This factor measures the rate at which earnings are generated by sales, in this case showing that 5 cents of every sales dollar is carried down to net income. This relationship will later govern the entire process of estab-

lishing the operating budget, since it specifies the required balancing of sales income against all costs and
expenses.

Return on Invested Capital: The Formula

These two factors—the turnover of capital and the
percentage of net earnings to sales—will, when brought
together, determine the rate of return on invested capital:

Turnover (2) × Earnings to sales (5%)
= Return on invested capital (10%)

From this it will be seen that the rate of return on
capital is a function of the *use* of capital (the dollar volume of sales that it can generate) and the *profitability* of
the volume managed (the net earnings as a percentage
of sales). Operating management must be concerned
with both, since neither by itself constitutes a final objective. Turnover alone, for example, might be increased
substantially by sharply reducing the prices charged for
the goods sold, thereby greatly increasing the dollar
volume of sales in relation to invested capital. If the
same action on price also resulted in a sharp drop in the
rate of net earnings to sales, however, the consequent
return on capital invested might well drop off and nothing would have been accomplished. In practice the
danger usually lies in the opposite direction.

Unless management is accustomed to measuring
these two factors together—one in conjunction with the
other—it will usually be motivated entirely in the direction of profits and may ignore the effect on invested

capital completely. Proposals, for example, aimed at increasing the rate of profits or earnings on sales will frequently entail the need for new equipment, additional warehouses, increased inventories, or extended trade receivables. Each of these represents a proposed increase in *assets* and—since assets ultimately must be supplied by invested capital—an increase in the level of capital itself. Too often the decisions are made solely on the basis of projected profits, even though the additional capital required may well result in such a low rate of turnover that the incremental rate of return on capital is considerably less than the cost of capital itself. In such a situation, the proposed action will result in a loss to the company, regardless of the accounted dollars of net profit.

The measurement of return on capital is thus seen as the interrelationship of the two key factors of turnover and rate of earnings, expressed as the following equation:

$$\frac{\text{Sales}}{\text{Capital}} \times \frac{\text{Earnings}}{\text{Sales}} = \text{Rate of return on capital}$$

From this, it will be noted that the factor for sales may be canceled out of the equation, leaving the original formula of earnings divided by average capital invested.

5

The Management
of Return on Capital

WHILE an understanding of the measurement of return on capital is obviously a prerequisite to its use as a
financial operating tool, it is the *management* of capital
that fulfills the basic role of financial management. The
management of capital will involve the management of
profit, and profit management, in turn, requires an
evaluation of the amount of profit needed to pay for the
cost of capital. It leads, in short, to the management of
the rate of return on invested capital.

A recognition of the cost of capital employed in a
business, the establishment of an operating goal in
terms of a desired rate of return on capital to cover such
cost and to provide an economic profit, and the ability to

accurately measure the results of operations and to report the rate of return on average capital invested are all
prerequisites to good financial planning. They do not,
however, constitute the *management* of capital.

Operating Tools in the
Management of Capital

The management of capital cannot be accomplished
by an after-the-fact calculation as measured in the final
casting up of the accounts, nor can it be accomplished by
periodic checks against the cumulative effect of decisions already taken in the operation of the business. To
be managed, the return-on-capital objective must be
used on a continuing basis throughout the decision-
making process and must be expressed in terms which
will lend themselves to a direct measurement of the
overall impact of each decision to be made. In the same
fashion that decisions on cost must be balanced against
the effects on production and that proposed changes in
the production schedule must be balanced against the
projected sales demands, each must, in turn, be balanced against the need for capital and the degree of risk
at which the capital will be employed. This can be done
only by use of the primary working tools of financial
management—the turnover of capital and the percentage of net earnings to sales. These two factors, which
support and determine the rate of return on invested
capital, are also the tools needed to plan and to manage
the use of capital.

In developing these subobjectives as operating tools
of the business, it will be seen not only that the ratio for
turnover and earnings on sales are closely related but

that the management of one will be completely dependent upon the management of the other. If, for example, a company had selected a 10 percent rate of return on invested capital as its basic financial objective, it would find a complete interdependence in the range of possible combinations of turnover and profit that would yield the desired rate of return on capital.

Turnover of Capital	×	Percent Profit Rate on Sales	=	Percent Rate of Return on Invested Capital
1.0		10.0		10.0
1.5		6.7		10.0
2.0		5.0		10.0
2.5		4.0		10.0
3.0		3.3		10.0
3.5		2.9		10.0
4.0		2.5		10.0
4.5		2.2		10.0
5.0		2.0		10.0

It would be evident, for example, that a rate of net earnings of only 2 percent on sales at a capital turnover of 5 *would result in exactly the same performance* as an earnings rate of 5 percent on a capital turnover of 2 and that a profit rate of 10 percent on sales would be required to match the rate of return on capital of either one if the turnover of capital were to drop to a ratio of 1:1. From this, it would also become evident that one measurement could not stand alone without the other and that, in fact, an objective for the percentage of profit or earnings on sales had no meaning whatsoever until it was linked to a corresponding objective for the turnover of capital. Conversely, it would also be seen that no increase in capital turnover could possibly compensate for an operating loss since both factors must have positive values if any return on capital is to be realized.

The mathematics of this relationship would permit an infinite series of combinations for any selected rate of return on capital. As shown in Exhibit 2, this could be constructed as a curve which would pinpoint the exact rate of turnover required for any given profit percentage or the exact rate of profit on sales demanded for any assumed level of capital turnover.

Adjusting and Balancing Turnover and Profit

From such an analysis, it will be seen that the management of return on capital calls for the simultaneous management of the two related factors of turnover and profit and that the two must be continuously managed *in combination* with one another if the overall results are to be achieved. If the objective set for the turnover of capital cannot be reached or maintained, then a corresponding increase in the profit rate of return on sales must be accomplished to maintain the proper balance between the two. If operating decisions or the forces of competition indicate a decline in the projected rate of profit, a compensating adjustment must be made to increase the rate of capital turnover. The management of return on capital thus becomes the task of *adjusting* and *balancing* the use of capital against the profit rate to meet the changing needs of the business.

The probable operating ranges or possible combinations of these two factors, however, will be found to be much more severely limited or restricted in practical application than the mathematics of the curve would

Exhibit 2

Relationship of Profit on Sales to Turnover of Capital

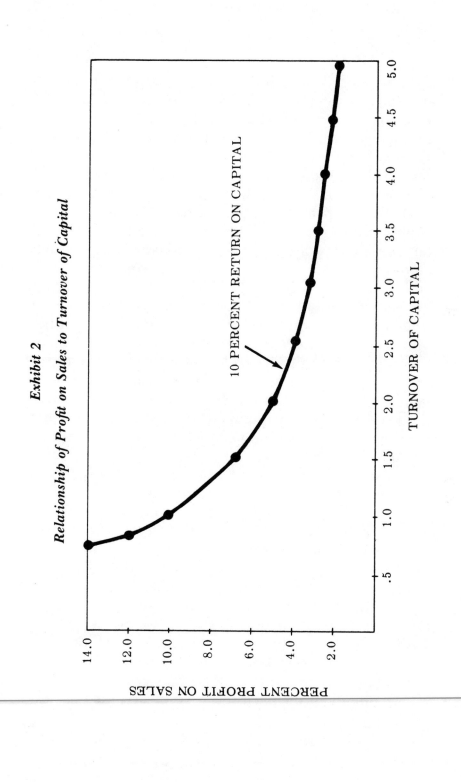

10 PERCENT RETURN ON CAPITAL

TURNOVER OF CAPITAL

PERCENT PROFIT ON SALES

suggest. They will be limited by the forces acting upon the business, forces which will effectively dictate the probable upper limits for each of these factors, establishing certain parameters which must be recognized before these tools can be put to work.

It will be seen that certain basic needs or requirements of the business itself would prohibit any arbitrary selection of a particular point on the curve or a random choice of these two multiples. Since the amount of capital employed will have a substantial bearing on the amount of profit that can be earned from operations, and since the use of capital will in turn have a significant impact on the cost of operations, the two factors have a leveling effect upon each other which tends to limit the optimum range or choice of combinations. The management of these two controls thus rests on the ability to find the point at which each will provide the greatest benefit to the other and to establish, at the same time, the probable limits or points of diminishing return beyond which further action would yield negative results.

The Measurement of Assets Employed

The inherent limitations on the rate of capital turnover and the rate of earnings on sales to be found in any single enterprise can perhaps be visualized more clearly if capital is thought of in its tangible form of assets employed. Capital is used to provide assets, and it is the assets themselves which support the operations and the level of volume to be produced and sold, so that the management of capital must, for operating purposes, be translated into the management of assets.

Among the principal assets used in a typical business

operation will be found the so-called *fixed assets* group of land, building, and machinery and the *current assets* or working capital elements of cash, inventory, and accounts receivable. Each of these has its own basic requirement or minimum investment which will place certain limitations or restrictions on the probable turnover of capital.

Fixed assets. The fixed assets group represents an investment of a somewhat permanent nature, and is perhaps rather adequately described since it is often "fixed" in more than accounting usage or terminology. An investment in land, buildings, and machinery represents a tie-up of capital which cannot readily be liquidated or adjusted over the short term. Once committed, it becomes a more or less immovable part of the capital structure and hence not subject to rapid change or variable adjustment. It contains, also, certain built-in minimum requirements that will dictate a basic level of investment simply to provide a foundation or operating capacity for the business, an investment which cannot easily be reduced to accommodate a change in the profit rate. This first layer of capital is thus largely locked in place and begins to place an upper limit on the probable turnover of total capital.

Current assets. The same will be found true, although to a lesser extent, in the basic investment needs for working capital. Although the turnover of cash, for example, may vary greatly from company to company depending on the operating objectives and the projected cash needs of the business, a certain minimum balance will be required to meet current payrolls, trade obligations, taxes, and the like. This minimum investment, while flexible to a certain degree and subject to short-term adjustment, will again add to the need for a basic level of capital employed and will further restrict the rate of capital turnover.

The turnover of capital funds tied up in accounts receivable will also be found to contain certain basic limitations. Very little business is transacted on the basis of immediate cash payment, and a planned volume of sales will, in most instances, depend entirely on the use of credit as part of the normal terms and conditions of sale. If, for example, goods were invoiced on payment terms of 30 days net, it would be quite likely that a minimum of 30 days' sales would be tied up in accounts receivable at all times, thus placing a *maximum* turnover rate of 12 times a year on this portion of the invested capital.

In the same fashion, a basic dollar investment in inventories will be an almost irreducible minimum in many operations. The funds required for investment in raw materials or supplies will be dictated both by availability and by economic lot size, while the length of the manufacturing cycle and the quantities required ahead of each operation will determine the level of investment required in the work-in-process inventory account. In addition, certain basic stocks of finished goods must be maintained in most business operations to satisfy the planned sales demand. The investment of capital funds in this area will often include minimum quantities consigned to quality inspection or testing in the plant, goods in transit, and inventories stocked in field warehouse locations. While increases in inventory investment may be controlled in direct proportion to anticipated increases in the dollar volume of sales (thus maintaining or possibly improving the turnover of inventory on a sales gain), the basic level of inventory investment required is seldom capable of any substantial reduction when sales volume decreases and thus constitutes one more element of capital for which a maximum rate of turnover is indicated.

Operating Limitations

The second set of conditions that will serve to place effective limits on the management of rate of return on capital will be found on the operating side or in the range of the probable rate of profit on sales. Price, for example, will be found to be a function of the basic value added in the process of manufacture and will ultimately be directed by customer demand and by competitive action to an optimum price/volume relationship. On the cost side of the ledger, various charges for depreciation, maintenance, occupancy, and warehousing will already have been set in motion by the decisions taken on the amount of capital employed and the use to which the capital funds were put in providing the assets of the business. These, in turn, will determine the probable level of other basic costs such as administration and supervision and many of the related overhead accounts.

In short, the needs of the business which dictated a certain basic or minimum investment of capital will also dictate a basic level of relatively fixed charges or time-oriented expenses required simply to maintain the operating capacity for the planned level of production and sales volume. It is the combination of these two forces that will work together to place practical operating limits on the rate of capital turnover and on the probable rate of earnings on the sales dollar.

Beyond the structure of the individual business, these limitations will be further solidified by the charac-

teristics of the industry itself. Here both the aggregate
effect of the forces already described and the nature of
the industry or type of business involved will combine to
form a pattern which will again narrow the choice of the
operating factors of turnover and profit.

The key to the configuration or profile typical for
any one industry will generally be found in the degree
of value added, whether it be value added in the process
of manufacture or value added by marketing and distribution. As has been noted, the amount of value added
to the basic raw materials used will govern the ultimate
relationship of price to cost. The higher the value
added, the greater, in general, will be the probability of
higher profits and the resulting rate of net earnings as a
percent of sales. The ability to add a substantial value to
the basic raw materials used, however, normally carries
with it a high degree of research and technology,
coupled with a substantially high investment in facilities
and equipment required for the processing or distribution of the product. The higher rate of return on sales is
therefore generally linked with a lower rate of capital
turnover for such an industry, establishing as it were a
normal set of conditions or combinations of operating
factors at one end of the spectrum.

By contrast, industries engaged primarily in assembly operations or in the mass distribution of basic com-
modities add very little value to the basic parts or materials used. As a consequence, the profit margins in such
industries are considerably lower, and an adequate return on invested capital must depend much more heavily on a higher rate of capital turnover. Since the lower
value-added products generally require less technology
and consequently far less capital investment in processing facilities and equipment, the lower profit rate on

sales can generally be combined with a relatively high turnover of invested capital—again resulting in the required rate of return on capital, but with a combination of operating factors representing the opposite end of the spectrum. The heavy industry group might typically operate with a capital investment roughly equal to the volume of sales for a turnover rate of around 1, but with a profit rate approaching a level of some 10 percent after taxes on the sales dollar. Companies engaged primarily in assembly operations or in mass distribution can manage an equally successful business with profit rates as low as 1 percent or less coupled with a capital turnover of 10 or higher. In between, the average industrial business will find that normal industry figures will be centered around a capital turnover rate of 2 combined with a profit rate of approximately 5 percent on sales.

Use of Guidelines

Since such figures describe only the general *averages* to be found in industry, they do not constitute acceptable goals or objectives for any one particular business. As averages, however, they do provide useful guidelines in establishing the probable limits around which any particular set of operations should be planned. It would not be feasible, for example, in a heavy industry to attempt to compensate for a sharp drop in the profit rate by a doubling or tripling of the rate of capital turnover. Nor would it be likely that a heavy tie-up of capital in commodity distribution could be offset by any substantial changes in price or cost. The basic nature of the business will already have established the upper limits

for each, and the economics of the enterprise will dictate
that the optimum combination must be found within a
fairly narrow range.

Optimizing the Use of Capital

The limitations thus placed upon the practical
operating range for the turnover of capital and for the
rate of earnings on sales in no way diminishes the importance or the value of these two factors as the operating tools of financial management. The very fact that
the range is limited, on the contrary, provides the
greatest incentive to management to fully utilize these
tools in the process of forward planning and in day-to-
day operations. It is, in other words, precisely *because*
such basic limitations do govern the use of capital and
the possibility of profits that the management of the rate
of return on capital must be developed to the point
where maximum leverage can be brought to bear. Since
the range is narrow, it is only by optimizing the use of
capital to produce the highest possible volume with the
lowest possible investment—and by combining these two
actions with an optimum rate of profit—that the concept
of the management of capital will be fully utilized.

The opportunities for such management will exist
primarily in the ongoing areas of decision making
where *changes* in the level of investment are proposed.
Since the basic level of capital required for the business
structure itself may offer little if any opportunity for
adjustment, it is in the rate and amount of change in the
use of assets during the life of the enterprise that the
management of capital will provide the greatest opportunities for balancing the changing pattern of income

and expense against the level of capital employed. Here, the proposals for investment in new plant and equipment, for increased inventories, or for extending the payment terms on trade receivables must each be measured against the projected gains in volume and operating profit, with each decision and each action weighed not only in terms of operating gains but in relation to the turnover of capital employed.

6

The Management
of Turnover

AS one-half of the equation that governs and controls
the rate of return on invested capital, turnover cannot
be managed as a separate entity in isolation from the
management of profit. Until it is linked to the profit rate
on sales, it has no particular value or meaning and must
be regarded as no more than a single element in a series
of control measurements. It does, however, deserve
separate treatment and separate analysis if for no other
reason than the fact that it is so frequently overlooked
or ignored.

The attention of operating management is often focused almost entirely on the more dynamic factors—

sales and production, schedules and deliveries—and on the current profit results of income and expense. This almost complete preoccupation with volume and profits can and in many companies frequently does lead to a series of decisions which ignores the use of capital employed. The drive for higher sales volume, efforts to increase the total dollars of net profit, and the goal of a continual increase in the reported book earnings per share all combine to push the individual operating elements forward in a unilateral fashion, often putting them out of balance with other control factors. Where the use of additional capital is not considered and measured in terms of the turnover rate for each separate increment, the apparent operating gains can actually result in a dilution of the earning power of the company or even in a gradual loss of capital itself.

A Common Misunderstanding

This weakness in the management of capital often stems from a lack of understanding concerning the nature of invested capital itself and the use to which capital is put in the current operations of a business. Since the term "capital" describes the *source* of the funds employed, it often takes on an abstract meaning having to do with outside financing, new stock issues, or the negotiation of loan agreements in the form of notes or bonds.

Such activities are remote and intangible to the average operating manager, and they often have no apparent relation to decisions needed on new equipment, the level of inventories, or the collection of accounts receivable. The general attitude may be that the company already *has* its capital, that the cash is already there or will be generated from profits, or that, in effect, it makes no difference how much capital is used since the cost of capital is not charged to the operating statement and thus has no apparent bearing on reported profits.

To use the measurement of capital turnover as a tool for management control, several steps are needed to change such attitudes and to bring the concept of the cost and use of capital into phase with current operating decisions. The first and foremost step is the fundamental one of linking profits to capital by reporting and measuring the profit results for each operation as a rate of return on the capital employed. The second step is to translate the use of capital into the use of *assets* and to develop an understanding on these three points: (1) that an increase in assets employed is, in effect, an increase of capital; (2) that capital in the form of assets must be put to work at the highest possible rate of utilization; and (3) that one measurement of such utilization is the rate of turnover of the dollars invested in assets.

Increase in Assets Equivalent to an Increase in Capital

While it is true that the movement of funds from one asset category to another will not, in itself, change the total level or amount of capital employed, it does not follow that the acquisition of assets in the form of buildings, equipment, or inventory is simply an internal use of a fixed amount of capital. If it were, it would mean that management could agree to a series of investment proposals for new equipment, for example, without regard for the cost of capital as long as the company had sufficient cash on hand to finance the acquisition.

Once the available cash had been used up, however, the next and equally sound proposal for another piece of new equipment would then have to be measured by different ground rules. For this next proposal and for others that would follow, the company would then have to go out and raise new capital and would thus assess a cost of capital charge against each subsequent proposal for investment in assets. Such a first-come, first-served approach is obviously neither workable nor useful, yet companies have at times followed such a course in the approval of capital budgets.

Since it is obvious that the aggregate of many investment decisions over a period of time can require additional outside capital, good financial management will regard *each* acquisition or proposed increase in assets as equivalent to an increase in capital and will measure each proposal in terms of the cost of capital employed. To carry this out effectively, each proposed change in the use of assets must be weighed against two factors—the incremental rate of net earnings on sales and the incremental rate of investment turnover. Since the two are completely interdependent, however, no separate standards or yardsticks can be developed or established for either. If, for example, a company were currently earning 10 percent on its invested capital through a combination of a turnover rate of 2 and a 5 percent rate of net earnings on sales, it could not afford to impose these individual rates as the sole measurement of each new proposal under consideration. If the turnover rate of 2 were to be used in judging the merits of each new investment in assets, for example, the following proposal would be turned down:

	Sales	Earn-ings	Capital	Turn-over	Per-cent Earn-ings	Per-cent Return on Capital
Present	$ 88,000	$4,400	$44,000	2.0	5.0	10.0
Proposed	12,000	1,200	8,000	1.5	10.0	15.0
Combined	$100,000	$5,600	$52,000	1.9	5.6	10.8

Turnover—A Relative Measure

If the proposed action in this example were sound, the incremental rate of return of 15 percent on capital would obviously represent a gain for the company in spite of the fact that the added investment would slow down the turnover rate of total capital employed. Turnover is thus seen as a *relative* measure to be used in conjunction with the measurement of profit and as a check on the adequacy of profits themselves. The use of turnover as a financial control will perhaps be seen more readily in a situation where the added dollars of profit are not adequate to support the added investment and where the proposed action does not justify the risk of capital in proposing an incremental rate of return which is less than the cost of capital itself. This can be demonstrated by coupling the projected earnings rate of 10 percent with a substantially higher level of incremental investment:

	Sales	Earn-ings	Capital	Turn-over	Per-cent Earn-ings	Per-cent Return on Capital
Present	$ 88,000	$4,400	$44,000	2.0	5.0	10.0
Proposed	12,000	1,200	15,000	.8	10.0	8.0
Combined	$100,000	$5,600	$59,000	1.7	5.6	9.5

Under these circumstances, the measurement of capital turnover should lead to the following evaluation of the proposed investment:

- The projected rate of 8 percent on new capital is less than the cost of capital, and the proposal as it stands should be rejected.
- In order to maintain the existing rate of return for the company, the new proposal can justify no more than $12,000 in added investment at the projected rate of profit on sales.
- Since some added risk may be expected in the new venture, the targeted rate of return on capital *should be greater than the existing rate* of 10 percent—preferably offering an opportunity for something in the range of a 15 percent rate of return on capital. At a rate of 10 percent net earnings on sales, this would indicate a need for a turnover rate of at least 1.5 on the incremental investment, reducing the allowable level to a maximum of $8,000 for added capital investment.

On the basis of such an analysis, the proposal might then be returned for further study to see whether alternate solutions might be found to minimize the need for capital. Since the original proposal presumably included estimates of additional working capital required for inventories and accounts receivable as well as the proposed acquisition of equipment, ways might be found to reduce the projected need for higher inventory through the use of common parts or by shortening the planned manufacturing cycle to reduce the level required for work-in-process investment. Whatever the outcome, the appraisal of turnover would have been used to identify the specific area of weakness in the plan and to quantify the problem in measurable terms.

Sales Versus Invested Capital

Used in this fashion as a working tool of financial management, the management of turnover will be seen as the management of the combined factors of the dollar volume of sales on the one hand and the total dollars of invested capital on the other. Once the required rate of turnover has been established to match the corresponding rate of profit, the management of turnover becomes the task of balancing sales against investment or volume against capital employed. In the same fashion that the rate of return on capital may be managed through various combinations of turnover rate and profit rate, turnover itself can be managed through various combinations of sales and capital.

Two Alternate Approaches

If higher volume could be managed with the same capital base by increasing the utilization of equipment, by a more efficient use of inventories, or by a faster collection of accounts receivable, the improvement in the turnover rate might be projected as follows:

Sales	÷	Capital	=	Turnover
$1,000		$1,000		1.0
1,500		1,000		1.5
2,000		1,000		2.0
2,500		1,000		2.5

If, on the other hand, higher sales volume did not appear probable because of the level of market demand, the same rate of improvement in turnover could be managed by reducing the need for capital through more effective utilization of assets while maintaining a constant sales base:

Sales	÷	Capital	=	Turnover
$1,000		$1,000		1.0
1,000		666		1.5
1,000		500		2.0
1,000		400		2.5

It will be noted that the combinations of sales and capital shown in these two alternate approaches result in exactly the same rate of turnover when each of the four steps is compared, so that a gain in turnover could be accomplished either through higher sales with the same capital or through a constant level of sales with reduced capital. If the rate of earnings on sales were the same in either case, it would then make no immediate difference which approach was chosen since the net rate of return on invested capital would be identical. As a practical matter, however, the choice of higher sales volume—if such a choice could arbitrarily be made—would be the more logical path to follow since it would normally offer a higher rate of profit because the associated costs would contain a lower proportion of fixed charges. In addition, the higher volume would mean growth, either as part of an expanding market or as a larger share of a mature market, and growth is obviously regarded as the more desirable approach to follow if it can be managed profitably.

Applicable Situations

While such a hypothetical example serves to illustrate the use of turnover in establishing the relationship of volume to capital, the instances in which this type of analysis may be used are by no means confined to situations where the choice is so obvious. It will often find its greatest use in decisions involving new products or new markets where projected sales, profit, and investment schedules must be tested for probability or in decisions concerning the continuance of marginal operations where the required rate of turnover can be used as a check against the estimated rate of return on capital.

The forces that control the rate of turnover of capital have already been described, suggesting the existence of certain upper limits or probable maximum rates of turnover for a particular industry. If, for example, it appeared that the highest turnover rate that might reasonably be expected for a particular operation was 2.5, this measurement could then be used to test the feasibility of a projected return of 15 percent on capital. Such a combination would thus demand an earnings rate of 6 percent after taxes on the dollar volume of sales. The probability of earning 6 percent on sales could therefore be checked against past records of the price/cost relationship or measured against the needs for cost reduction, volume increase, or higher prices required to meet such an objective. In other situations, the continuance of a marginal income operation might be defended on the grounds that it contributed *something* to profits and thus helped to improve the reported earnings per share. If the projected profit, for example, could not be expected to produce more than a 1 percent rate of return on sales, a turnover rate of 10 would be required to yield the 10 percent return that would justify the risk of the capital employed.

Turnover Rate as a Working Tool

While the turnover of capital can thus be used as an element of financial measurement and control, its use as a working tool of operating management will require that it be broken down into a series of subgoals and subobjectives in which the concept can be applied to specific segments of the capital structure. The management of capital is essentially the management of *assets*, and by the same token the turnover of capital will be made up of a series of individual turnover rates for each element of the assets employed. These individual rates will then be found to be interrelated and interdependent, since they must be fitted together in various combinations which will satisfy the aggregate need for the turnover of total assets and total capital.

A Typical Balance Sheet

The development of the subobjectives for the turnover of the asset accounts can best be illustrated by the use of a typical balance sheet presentation as shown on page 84.

Assuming annual sales of $20,000, the company would be achieving a total turnover rate of 2, based either on the total capital of $10,000 as reported on the balance sheet or on the total assets of $12,000 minus the operating debt of $2,000—since the net amount of invested capital may be determined by either method. In order to break down or subdivide the overall rate of

Assets		*Liabilities*	
Current Assets:		*Current Liabilities:*	
Cash	$ 500	Accounts Payable	$ 1,000
Accounts Receivable	2,500	Accrued Payroll	500
Inventory	5,000	Accrued Taxes	500
Total Current Assets	$ 8,000	Total Current Liabilities	$ 2,000
Fixed Assets:		*Invested Capital:*	
Land and Buildings	$ 2,000	Long-Term Debt	$ 2,000
Equipment (net of depreciation)	2,000	Capital Stock	4,000
		Retained Earnings	4,000
Total Fixed Assets	$ 4,000	Total Capital	$10,000
		Total Liabilities	
Total Assets	$12,000	*and Capital*	$12,000

turnover on total capital into the individual turnover rates for assets employed, the following analysis would be made:

$$\frac{\text{Sales } \$20,000}{\text{Cash } 500} = \text{Turnover } 40.0$$

$$\frac{\text{Sales } \$20,000}{\text{Accounts receivable } 2,500} = \text{Turnover } 8.0$$

$$\frac{\text{Sales } \$20,000}{\text{Inventory } 5,000} = \text{Turnover } 4.0$$

$$\frac{\text{Sales } \$20,000}{\text{Fixed assets } 4,000} = \text{Turnover } 5.0$$

$$\frac{\text{Sales } \$20,000}{\text{Total assets } 12,000} = \text{Turnover } 1.7$$

$$\frac{\text{Sales } \$20,000}{\text{Operating debt } 2,000} = \text{Turnover } (10.0)$$

$$\frac{\text{Sales } \$20,000}{\text{Capital } 10,000} = \text{Turnover } 2.0$$

From this analysis, the overall corporate control on the turnover of capital can be translated into operational control for the turnover of assets. The analysis of each element of the asset structure would then entail the following:

Cash. At a turnover of 40 times, one dollar in the average cash balance is supporting forty dollars of annual sales volume. At turnover rates well below forty the low turnover is evidence of idle cash, while turnover rates much higher than forty would indicate a probable shortage of cash with a consequent delinquency in payables.

Accounts Receivable. The turnover rate of 8 is equal to one and one-half months' or 45 days' sales tied up in receivables. The targeted turnover for receivables might be raised to 12 if all accounts could be collected within 30 days, or it might be found closer to 6 if the terms and conditions of sales were extended to an average collection period of 60 days.

Inventory. The turnover of 4 computed for the investment of $5,000 in inventory represents the rate of turnover of *dollars* and not the physical usage or turnover of the inventory in terms of the number of weeks' supply on hand. If accepted as a manageable goal for total inventory, the turnover of 4 should then be further subdivided into separate targets for each element of inventory, with individual turnover rates set for raw materials, work in process, and finished goods.

Fixed Assets. The turnover rate of 5 for the total

investment in plant and equipment should be checked against the utilization of capacity before being accepted as a proper target. Once a goal has been set at close to 100 percent of capacity in terms of physical quantities of production, it will be found that further efforts to improve the turnover of fixed asset investment will be largely dependent on increases in selling price.

Total Assets. The turnover of 1.7 on total assets as opposed to a turnover of 2 for total capital employed reflects the normal relationship of assets to capital and describes a subgoal which can be used at the plant or divisional level of the company.

Operating Debt. The turnover of (10) is essentially a measurement of the management of the payables, with a lower turnover indicating a stretch-out of payables and higher turnover rates a possible pre-payment of amounts due.

Turnover Rates in Planning, Budgeting, and Forecasting

Once established, the turnover rates or goals for each of the asset accounts can be put to use as working tools in at least three principal areas of financial management. In planning, budgeting, and forecasting, the targeted rates of asset turnover will be found useful in projecting the *allowable* or desired levels of investment in relation to the planned dollar volume of sales. On projected sales of $120,000, for example, an inventory turnover target of 6 would dictate a maximum investment of $20,000, a figure which could then be broken into allowable totals for each of the inventory elements and made a part of a balanced plan for operations. Against this projected investment, the probability or feasibility of carrying out the proposed production plan with $20,000 worth of inventory could next be analyzed. If it were then found, for example, that the projected *needs* for inventory would exceed the allowable level, the turnover rates would then be put to their second use in financial control.

This second use will go hand in hand with the first, since it is simply the use of the turnover measurement for *compensating* or adjusting the several individual rates within the asset structure itself. On the assumption that the goal for the *total* turnover of capital is still adequate to match the rate of earnings on sales, the total turnover must be maintained to provide the planned rate of return on capital. If, however, slippage has occurred or has been indicated for one of the asset elements such as inventory, a *compensating adjustment* must be made in the turnover rate for one of the other asset accounts. The turnover of accounts receivable or the turnover of dollars invested in plant and equipment must now be improved to maintain the required rate of turnover for the group as a whole. This will involve a series of analyses in the possible areas for corrective action. If none can be found, attention must then be directed to the profit rate itself as a means of compensating for the slowdown in the turnover rate of total capital.

This, in turn, will lead to the third use of the turnover rates in maintaining a balanced financial plan for operations. The two previous steps have assumed a constant rate of earnings on sales, a factor which necessitated no more than the maintenance of the turnover rate on total capital or the readjustment of the individual asset turnover targets themselves. The third use of the management of turnover will be found when the profit rates cannot be maintained and where the demand for an adequate return on invested capital dictates a need for greater turnover of total capital to compensate for a decline in profits.

7

The Management
of Profit

IN the final analysis, the management of turnover is the management of but one element in a series, each of which must be coordinated and balanced with the others. The primary element, however, which will govern the management of turnover is the management of profit itself.

Management of Unit Volume

The management of profit involves the simultaneous management of the three interrelated factors of volume, cost, and price. Of the three, the management of unit volume is perhaps the simplest and the one most readily managed.

Since good operating management will require that the level of production be kept in balance with the level of sales over a period of time, the management of volume is essentially the management of the rate of production. Although many factors will dictate frequent and unexpected changes in the short-term volume and mix of production, the long-term management of profitable production will depend almost entirely on the proper management of assets. In a broad sense, these assets will include the investment in time and people as well as the more specific dollar investments in materials and equipment.

In a narrower sense, profitable production management will rest largely on the use of capital invested in machines and equipment. This use of capital has provided a certain level of operating capacity, and the cost of maintaining such capacity is reflected both in the cost of the capital employed and in the supporting costs for supervision, maintenance, insurance, taxes, and the like. Unless this capacity is used effectively, such costs will not be fully recovered, and production will be less than profitable. In short, the profit management of physical volume can be translated into the management of capacity. This is usually expressed in terms of *utilization of capacity,* with effectiveness normally measured as a percentage attainment of rated capacity.

Capacity as optimum value. The measurement of capacity itself is often difficult and subject to change with the mix of production, the availability of labor, or the need for machine changeover and maintenance. For this reason, capacity must be defined in terms of *optimum* rather than maximum volume. Since the crossover point in effective utilization of capacity will usually be found at some point well short of a three-shift seven-day operation, for example, the optimum level of capacity may frequently be placed at the volume attainable on a two-shift operation for a normal five-day workweek. Once defined, the profitable range of utilization of capacity must then be determined in order to plan properly for profit effectiveness. This can best be done by construction of a breakeven chart, such as the one shown in Exhibit 3. Because volume is plotted in increments of productive capacity, the breakeven chart identifies the profit leverage to be obtained as volume passes the breakeven point.

From such an analysis, it will be seen that operations at 50 percent of capacity would, in this example, provide only a sufficient volume of production and sales to recover the total of the fixed and variable costs, resulting in zero profit or *breakeven performance*. It will also be seen, however, that operations above the breakeven level provide an immediate profit and that the profit leverage increases rapidly as the utilization of rated capacity approaches 100 percent. Since the rate of incremental profit or marginal contribution will be a function of the rate of incremental or variable costs, the management of volume will thus depend, in turn, on the second factor of profit management: the analysis and management of cost.

Cost Management

Cost management is generally regarded as the *control* of costs or the ability of management to hold costs within the limits established by the operating budget.

Exhibit 3

Breakeven Chart

Basic to the concept of cost control, however, is the need to recognize the existence of different cost elements in a business structure and to understand the different patterns of *cost behavior* that will be found in each element. The ability to manage costs will thus depend to a large extent on how the various costs and expenses themselves are categorized, how they are measured and evaluated, and how they are reported and analyzed in the financial statements presented to operating management. The classification, analysis, and reporting of costs will, in turn, depend almost entirely on the choice of an accounting system, since the system itself will normally reflect the attitudes of management toward cost control and will become the basis for profit planning and profit management.

Absorption Costing

There are many types of accounting systems in use in business operations, but all of them rest on one of two basic approaches or fundamental *methods* of cost accounting. The first and oldest method is generally described as a concept of *absorption costing,* a method whereby all costs are absorbed into a unit of production or charged against a single product or operation within the business.

This concept rests on the theory that all costs *belong* to some particular segment of the output, that each operation must carry a *share* of the several cost elements, and that the indirect or supporting elements of the cost structure should be *allocated* or distributed by various methods to reflect an assumed "total cost" for each unit of production, each product or product line, or each sales territory or market. In doing so, absorption accounting assumes that all costs are essentially alike, that they will respond in similar fashion to changes in the level of operations, and that they can be measured and controlled by a single overall method or approach to cost management.

Direct Costing

By contrast, the second or alternate basic choice of an accounting method treats the classification, analysis, and control of costs in an entirely different fashion. This method, generally described as *direct costing,* rests on one fundamental concept which makes it unique among accounting presentations. This is no more than simple recognition of the fact that there are two entirely different types of costs and expenses in a typical business operation, that the two groups exist for different purposes, that these two cost elements are diverse in nature and different in patterns of cost behavior, and that they must be measured and controlled by separate techniques.

Fixed costs. The first group consists of those costs and expenses which are considered necessary to support the business structure *even if nothing is produced or sold for a period of time.* These costs of simply being in business are variously described as "capacity costs," "fixed costs," or "period expenses." In essence, they are time-oriented in the sense that they are incurred as a function of time rather than as a function of volume. Included in this category would be such charges as depreciation, insurance, taxes, rent, salaries, and the like. Since these costs are created initially by management decision, and since they tend to continue at predictably constant levels until changed by further management decisions, they are recognized as being separate and distinct from the variable costs of production. Under direct costing, they are not unitized in the cost of production and not carried in the product inventory valuation but are planned, controlled, and measured on a "spending" basis in original totals rather than being fragmented and dispersed through a system of overhead rate allocations.

Variable costs. The second group of costs consists of those cost elements which are shown by analysis to vary in direct proportion to the volume of goods produced or the volume of goods sold. In a manufacturing operation, these costs would typically include direct materials, direct labor, and the fringe-benefit costs associated with direct labor, together with other such items of variable overhead expense that might bear a linear relationship to volume. In the marketing area, direct costs are normally confined to such items as sales commissions—costs which vary directly with the dollar volume of goods sold. Taken in the aggregate, the total direct costs are recognized as costs whose levels, for the near term, are not established by management decision. Instead, these costs are set in motion by the external forces of the marketplace that determine the volume of goods to be produced and the volume of goods to be sold for a given period of time. Such costs are not budgeted and controlled at a predetermined spending level, but are properly planned and measured on the basis of units of production or as a function of the dollar volume of sales.

In short, both cost elements—the fixed or period expenses of being in business, and the direct or variable costs of production and sales—are *controllable,* but are planned, controlled, and evaluated by entirely different techniques.

As a result of this separation of fixed and variable costs, the presentation of financial statements on the basis of direct costing affords an immediate determination of breakeven point volume—a control measure which involves the continual monitoring of all decisions taken in the area of period expenses, direct variable costs, productive capacity, planned volume, and price. Any action taken in these segments of the operation will—either singly or in combination—have an effect on the breakeven point. Control must be exercised to insure that the cumulative effect of such decisions does not adversely affect the desired margin of safety over breakeven volume.

Such control rests upon (1) a proper interpretation of the behavior pattern of the various cost elements being measured and (2) the means for ready identification and appraisal of the several segments of the direct and period expense structures. An analysis of this type cannot readily be made by a review of overhead rates or by a reexamination of the methods used for allocating fixed charges. It can, however, be made with relative ease from an operating statement or forecast prepared on the basis of direct costing. The breakeven point calculation can be made directly from the financial statement by simply dividing the total of all period expenses by the marginal contribution percentage to gross sales. This latter measurement is the profit-to-volume or P/V ratio, a midpoint value which can often become a key control point for profit leverage.

The Standard Cost Approach

The management of cost can be further enhanced by refining the measurement and evaluation of the cost figures from an accumulation of historical recorded costs to a statement of what costs ought to be for a given level of output. This approach to cost management, the use of *standard cost,* has long been recognized as an effective means of planning, controlling, and measuring cost performance. By establishing values of *what the costs should be* for a given set of conditions, the differences between such predetermined costs and subsequent actual results can be expressed in terms of *cost variances,* which make it possible to report significant items and trends on an exception basis. The value of such an analysis, however, depends entirely on the substance and meaning of the reported variances. Under a standard cost system based on the principle of full overhead absorption, for example, the measure of *volume variance* is not subject to cost control since it represents no more than the overabsorption or underabsorption of fixed overhead as compared with a planned rate of allocation at a different level of production. When this type of "variance," in turn, is distributed to product or unit costs, the need for corrective action on a particular product line is often obscured by the accounting procedure. In short, the reported figures can frequently vary more from accounting treatment than they will from actual changes in efficiency and production performance.

A more effective use of standard costs will be found when they are limited to the direct variable costs of production as defined under a direct costing system. Once divorced from any relationship with the fixed or period expense elements, the standards for direct materials, direct labor, and variable overhead can, if properly developed, provide a statement of predetermined costs which will remain constant per unit of production at any level of volume within the capacity limits and which will be entirely free of the effect of over- or underabsorbed burden. Variances from such standards will then provide a direct correlation between cost and performance and will indicate clearly the effectiveness of cost control by cost element.

In like fashion, each of the period expenses reported will stand apart from the production measurement, and each will be held and reported in total for each category of expense for measurement against the amount planned or budgeted. Cost control in this area will also become more effective, since the fixed expenses will be measured directly against a "spending" budget instead of being adjusted mathematically for purported "cost allowances" based on changes in production volume.

These points can best be illustrated in the presentation of a typical profit and loss statement prepared on the basis of standard direct costing in which operating results have been broken out by product line and each element of income and expense has been compared with the financial budget for the period. (See Exhibit 4.)

It will be noted that several key factors are highlighted for immediate analysis in a direct costing presentation of this type:

- Changes from budgeted volume in the two product lines have produced predictable results, with the standard margin on sales for each product line changing in direct proportion to the increase or decrease in the level of sales income. Had price changes also occurred, or had a shift in type mix within either of the product lines taken place, the effect of such deviations from plan would then have been reflected in the rate of marginal contribution, and the profit impact of each could have been isolated and measured.

- Although total sales volume of $10,000 is exactly on budget for the period, profit has fallen 33 percent to a level of $805 before taxes. The fall-off of $395 is immediately attributable to three factors:
    1. A drop of $125 in the standard margin on sales as a result of a shift in sales mix between product lines A and B.
    2. Poor manufacturing efficiency in product line B, as evidenced by the operating variance of $125.
    3. A net increase of $145 in period expenses over the total of $4,800 budgeted.
- Those elements of period expense which exist solely for the support of a single product line, which are not common to the business as a whole, and which could be eliminated in their entirety if the product line were discontinued, are segregated in the operating statement as "assignable period expense." The resulting measure of "product-line contribution" provides a figure indicating the relative profitability of the several product lines at varying levels of volume. This becomes a vital tool in planning and in optimizing the use of productive capacity.
- Breakeven point volume has climbed from a budgeted level of $8,000 to an actual rate of $8,600 for the period, as calculated directly from the operating statement:

Exhibit 4

Operating Statement Prepared According to Standard Direct Costing Methods

	Product A		Product B		Total	
	Budget *3,000* *Units*	*Actual* *2,500* *Units*	*Budget* *4,000* *Units*	*Actual* *5,000* *Units*	*Budget* *7,000* *Units*	*Actual* *7,500* *Units*
Average Price	$2.00	$2.00	$1.00	$1.00	$1.43	$1.33
Gross Sales	$6,000	$5,000	$4,000	$5,000	$10,000	$10,000
Deductions	120	100	80	100	200	200
Net Sales	5,880	4,900	3,920	4,900	9,800	9,800
Standard Direct Cost of Sales:						
Manufacturing	1,800	1,500	1,600	2,000	3,400	3,500
Selling	180	150	220	275	400	425
Total Standard Direct Cost	1,980	1,650	1,820	2,275	3,800	3,925

						Total
Standard Margin on Sales	3,900	3,250	2,100	2,625	6,000	5,875
Operating Variances	—	—	—	125	—	125
Net Marginal Contribution	3,900	3,250	2,100	2,500	6,000	5,750
P/V Ratio	65.0%	65.0%	52.5%	50.0%	60.0%	57.5%
Assignable Period Expense:						
Manufacturing	1,700	1,700	400	425	2,100	2,125
Research and Development	300	300	50	50	350	350
Marketing	100	100	50	60	150	160
Total Assignable	2,100	2,100	500	535	2,600	2,635
Product-Line Contribution	1,800	1,150	1,600	1,965	3,400	3,115
Nonassignable Period Expense						
Manufacturing					900	965
Research and Development					200	190
Marketing					550	575
Administrative					550	580
Total					$ 2,200	$ 2,310
Profit Before Taxes					$ 1,200	$ 805

	Budget	Actual
Assignable Period Expense	$2,600	$2,635
Nonassignable Period Expense	2,200	2,310
Total Period Expense	$4,800	$4,945
Divided by P/V Ratio	60.0%	57.5%
Breakeven Volume	$8,000	$8,600

The profit deviation from plan is thus clearly identified as to cause, and the specific corrective action needed to bring results back in line with the operating plan is indicated directly on the profit and loss statement itself.

The visibility afforded by the use of direct costing will become even more apparent when figures are needed for a series of make-or-buy decisions. Such decisions must be based on an appraisal of whether certain parts or components can be purchased more cheaply than they can be manufactured in house, and while the evaluation is usually precise as to the purchased cost for a given quantity, it is often vague or misleading where predicted internal costs are concerned. A valid choice must be based upon *estimates of incremental cost,* including the cost of any additional increments of capital required. A clear understanding of incremental costs is often difficult to reach under an absorption system of accounting, since both the historical and projected unit costs will normally include several allocations or layers of allocations of fixed overhead. The question to be answered in a make-or-buy decision is not what costs "belong" to a certain part or component—the traditional viewpoint of older systems of cost accounting—but what the total costs of the operation will be both with and without the manufacture of the proposed article.

A Direct Costing Analysis

This determination of cost will be readily apparent from a direct costing analysis. Direct variable costs can be estimated for each element of materials, direct labor, and the related items of variable overhead expense. Once properly defined and measured, this estimate can be used to provide a constant measure of the unit cost of production which will determine the in-house cost to manufacture. A second and separate step to be taken is an estimate of additional or incremental costs to be incurred in the period expense group in support of the additional production, together with an estimate of the cost of capital to be incurred in providing additional fixed assets or working capital. The aggregate of these incremental overheads should then—and for this purpose only—be divided by the total unit quantity planned for production in the same period of time, and the unitized results should be added to the direct variable or constant unit cost to arrive at a total cost to be compared with the outside purchase price. In following this procedure, it is worth noting that the period expenses are unitized only for purposes of a one-time decision-making process and that, once the decision has been made to produce the article and to incur the added costs, such items would not thereafter be unitized in the accounting reports.

Direct costing will also offer several distinct advantages for internal reporting and control when standard direct costing is used as the basis for the valuation of inventories:

- Since all fixed overhead is charged directly to the income statement for the period, the reported operating profit is in no way affected by the deferral of fixed cost into inventory. This results in a direct correlation between sales volume and reported profit and makes it impossible to show a fictitious book "profit" from high production—a situation which frequently serves to cover up poor sales performance under some systems of absorption costing.

- With all operating variances also charged directly against income for the period, operating performance has a direct impact on the current financial statement and is not deferred through inventory to a later period.
- Stripped of fixed-cost allocations and operating variances charged to the inventory account, a constant valuation at a predetermined standard direct cost per unit provides a uniform and predictable flow of cost through the inventory account and into the cost of goods sold. This, in turn, provides improved budgeting and forecasting accuracy in projecting the marginal contribution accruing to varying levels of sales volume.

For external reporting of financial information such as published earnings reports and tax returns, it is often necessary to "reconvert" the inventory values back to a full absorption cost valuation in order to maintain the continuity of reported profits on a basis consistent with prior years. This need should be secondary to the internal need for a management control system based on direct costing techniques and can be met without sacrificing the value of internal statements. It can be accomplished quite simply by computing the number of weeks or months required to produce the inventory on hand at the end of the period to be reported, then determining from the direct costing statement the total amount of manufacturing fixed overhead or period expense incurred over the same period of time. This latter amount is then booked in a lump sum as a net adjustment to total profits reported under direct costing, with the inventory valuation on the balance sheet increased by a corresponding amount. This element may be carried on the books in a separate account designated as the "fixed overhead value in inventory," and it can be adjusted either up or down in subsequent reporting periods.

Planning Estimates

The valuation of inventories at standard direct cost will have particular advantages in planning. Nowhere do the basic weaknesses of various systems of absorption costing become more apparent than in attempts to project current accounted results into the future. Whether the projection is a forecast for the following three months, a budget for the coming year, or a projection of operating results for a five-year plan, the difficulties encountered in determining probable cost levels in terms of overhead rates will be the same. As can be seen from the value of a direct costing analysis in the areas of current operating decisions, the technique lends both simplicity and understanding to the various elements of cost and expense. The same basic values will also add a considerable amount of meaning and clarity to the presentation of planning estimates—the effectiveness of which will depend to a large extent on management's grasp of the nature of the two fundamentally different types of cost involved in financial planning.

The management of cost will then set the stage for the third and final element of profit management—the management of pricing. Although pricing decisions are, quite frequently, based on competitive action rather than on the accumulation, analysis, or prediction of internal costs, a reference to cost information will be essential in gauging the profitability of following such competitive prices or in evaluating the consequences of pricing above or below the market. In doing so, no useful comparison can possibly be made unless the unit type costs can be relied upon as truly representative of the past or future cost of production. When such costs are based on a confused mixture of fixed and variable costs, and when under many systems of full-absorption accounting the reported figures are out of phase with current levels of volume, the resulting reported figures can contain serious distortions which can lead to substantial errors in pricing judgment.

Direct Costing Benefits

Direct costing offers three distinct and clear-cut benefits in the use of cost information for pricing:

1. Product or type costs are expressed in terms of direct variable cost only and contain no element of fixed overhead allocation. Unit costs are thus freed of dependence on volume and mix and are also independent of the effect of changes in the fixed or period expense structure itself. Since they are directly variable with volume, they can be regarded as *constant unit costs* within the framework of planned capacity. This will provide

a direct measure of marginal contribution per unit when measured against a proposed selling price. The results thus obtained will then hold true *at any level of unit volume* within the operating limits of plant capacity.

2. The margin per unit multiplied by the number of units to be produced and sold provides a measure of marginal contribution dollars which must (*a*) be sufficient to cover the aggregate of all period expenses and (*b*) leave a residue of profit which will provide an adequate return on capital.

3. With these two elements, an exact calculation of the price required to attain the profit objective can then be carried out in the following way:

   (a) Determine the amount of capital required to support the assumed level of operations. This would normally consist of present investment plus or minus anticipated changes in fixed asset and working-capital needs.

   (b) Define the pretax rate of profit required on invested capital and apply this rate to determine the dollars of profit required.

   (c) Determine the total amount of period expense required to support the planned level of operations and add this total to the profit requirement to determine the dollar amount of marginal contribution required from sales.

   (d) Multiply the assumed unit volume by the direct variable or constant unit cost of production to determine the standard direct cost of goods sold. Add this total to the dollars of marginal contribution required to arrive at the dollar value of sales.

(e) Divide the dollar value of sales by the number of units used in the previous calculations. This will provide the desired unit selling price which will meet the targeted rate of return on capital employed if the cost and volume estimates can be achieved.

This process of the "reverse engineering" of a profit and loss statement can then be developed for several assumed levels of unit volume within the limits of operating capacity to determine the range of prices required to meet the profit targets at various levels of volume. Assuming a rated capacity of 100,000 units of production, such an analysis might be presented as follows:

Unit Volume	20,000	60,000	100,000
Assets Employed:			
Fixed Assets	$ 50,000	$ 50,000	$ 50,000
Working Capital	50,000	65,000	75,000
Total Assets	100,000	115,000	125,000
Pretax Profit Required @ 30 Percent			
of Assets Employed	30,000	34,500	37,500
Period Expenses	90,000	103,500	112,500
Marginal Contribution Required	120,000	138,000	150,000
Direct Cost @ $1/Unit	20,000	60,000	100,000
Gross Sales	$140,000	$198,000	$250,000
Selling Price Required	$7.00	$3.30	$2.50

The Pricing Curve

By computing the prices required to satisfy the pretax profit requirement of a 30 percent return on assets employed at other intermediate points within the capac-

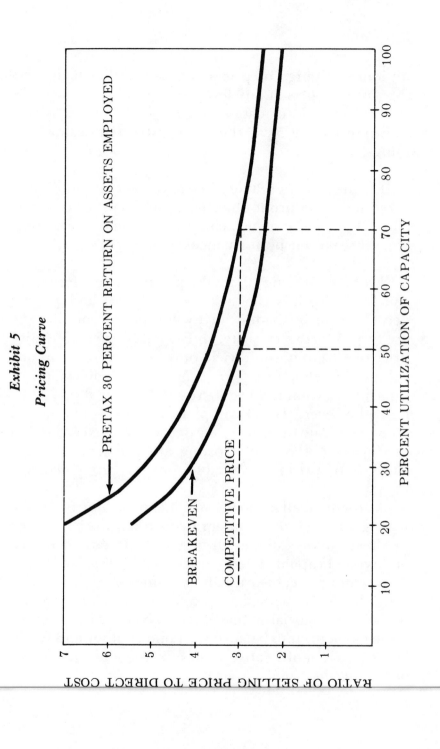

Exhibit 5
Pricing Curve

PRETAX 30 PERCENT RETURN ON ASSETS EMPLOYED

BREAKEVEN

COMPETITIVE PRICE

RATIO OF SELLING PRICE TO DIRECT COST

PERCENT UTILIZATION OF CAPACITY

ity limits, a range of prices can be developed to meet the profit targets at any level of volume.

From this information, a *pricing curve* such as that shown in Exhibit 5 can then be constructed to show two things:

1. The ratio of selling price to direct cost required to meet the profit objective at any level of capacity.
2. The ratio at which prices would yield only breakeven performance.

From the pricing curve, the profit impact of meeting competitive prices can next be analyzed, and pricing decisions can be made which will serve to optimize the use of productive capacity. In Exhibit 5, the competitive price of $3 a unit would yield only breakeven results at a volume of 50,000 units or a 50 percent utilization of capacity. If volume were increased to a total of 70,000 units, however, the $3 competitive price would yield a 30 percent rate of return on assets before taxes. Used in this manner, the direct costing analysis can make the vital job of pricing a valuable tool for profit management.

In the final analysis, the management of profit is the management of all the integrated forces which combine to affect the overall measurement of the rate of return on invested capital. The interaction of volume and cost, of cost and price, of price and volume—and of all three with the level of capital employed—provides an approach to financial management which brings each of these elements into balance with one another and establishes a system of relative values for the management of operating decisions.

8

The Need for Balanced
Financial Controls

THE successful management of the business enterprise
will depend, in the long run, on the ability to recognize
the interdependence of the operating and capital elements of the business structure and to achieve a *balanced
financial control* of operations. To reach this point, (1)
the role of financial management and the nature of invested capital must be fully understood by those having
the authority and the responsibility for decision making,
(2) the cost of capital employed in the business must be
defined and translated into specific objectives for profits
that will provide an adequate return on invested capital,
and (3) operating targets must be established for the
management of capital turnover and for the manage-

ment of profit rates that will support these basic objectives. To then maintain an orderly *balance* between these several elements, management must clearly identify the interrelationship between capital and profit and must develop an operating plan which fully recognizes the interdependence of the operating decisions themselves.

Interrelationship of Capital and Profit

How does capital affect profit and profit, capital? This question can best be answered by taking each element in the sequence in which it occurs in the development of the business structure.

Capital requires profits. From the inception of the business, the acceptance of capital funds from the investor places upon management a *requirement* to earn a profit that will justify the risk to which the capital has been put. Since the need for capital will continue throughout the life of the enterprise, the profit demand will be a continuing requirement which must become the primary goal of operating management.

Profits increase capital. Achievement of the first goal—earning a profit sufficient to justify the use of capital employed—will then generate additional funds, part of which may be returned to the investor in the form of dividends. Since dividend payments do normally represent only a portion of the earnings from operations, however, the bulk of the net earnings are usually retained in the business to finance future growth and expansion. These retained earnings are, in effect, additional capital, and successive increments of new capital will continue to be generated as long as operations remain profitable unless all the earnings are returned to the stockholders.

Higher capital requires higher profits. Yesterday's profit dollars are no longer sufficient to maintain the required profitability level. The initial capital has now been increased by the amount of the earnings retained in the business, and a corresponding *increase* in the level of profits will now be needed just to maintain an adequate rate of return on total capital employed.

Profits require more profits. The success of the business enterprise in earning enough profits to support the initial capital investment will, in itself, result in a continual increase in the total amount of capital employed. As capital increases, the profit requirement will also increase, with the result that profits themselves will ultimately call for even greater profits as the business continues to grow.

Need for Integration

From this, it will be seen that the process of financial management is a process of continual *adjustment* and that the changing needs and changing targets require more than a simple coordination of operating plans and decisions if the basic return-on-capital objective is to be maintained. Coordination implies a series of unilateral decisions and actions which must be checked at periodic intervals to insure that they are moving in the same general direction, that they do not conflict with one another, and that they conform to an overall plan or statement of objectives. The *coordination* of management functions is thus basically weak in that it tends either to rely on steps to *correct* decisions that do not serve to maintain a balanced control of objectives or to take action after the fact rather than on the basis of a prior evaluation of the specific steps required. The need is not for coordination, but for a complete *integration* of business decisions—a management plan which will recognize that each element of business operations, and hence each operating decision, is in fact completely integrated with and interdependent upon all other elements of the business. Thus no one decision of any significance can stand alone or be isolated in its impact on the structure as a whole. This can best be visualized by tracing, in Exhibit 6, the steps required to manage return on capital and by noting the interaction of the key elements involved.

Simultaneous Management of Turnover and Profit Rates

The return-on-capital objective must be managed through a combination of the turnover rate of capital employed and the profit rate—the percent of net earnings to sales. The management of each of these two controls will, in turn, involve the management of subgoals and individual operating functions which will be found to be completely interrelated, so that management of turnover will directly affect the management of the profit rate and vice versa.

The management of the turnover rate, for example, will include the following:

- The simultaneous management of the dollar volume of sales and the dollar level of capital invested, since turnover itself is a direct function of these two variables.

Exhibit 6

The Dynamics of Business Decisions

- The management of unit price and the management of productive capacity, since these two factors will determine the dollar volume of goods to be produced and sold.
- The management of volume and the management of the cost of maintaining and operating the capacity required to produce and market such volume, since both will affect the level of investment required.
- The management of income and expense, since these factors will be governed by the management of price, capacity, volume, and cost.
- The indirect management of the profit rate itself, since it in turn is a direct function of income and expense.

In summary, the factors required to manage the turnover rate of capital employed lead directly to the factors required to manage the profit rate on sales. It can also be seen that the factors which control the profit rate itself are identical, and, when approached from the opposite direction, they will lead directly to the management of turnover. The two are thus completely interwoven and demonstrate the need for a fully integrated plan for balanced financial planning and control.

Establishing Ratios

A completely balanced and integrated plan for the financial management of a business can be developed by this simple process: Establish a series of ratios or standards for each element to be controlled; identify the relationship of one element to another so as to put the entire structure of the business into complete perspective; manage it as a single entity through the simultaneous management of each of the several controlling elements. If, as in Exhibit 7, the short-term objective of a company were to earn a minimum of a 10 percent rate of return on invested capital, the financial plan for operations would start with this objective and would immediately proceed to describe the two primary standards by which the result might be achieved.

Exhibit 7

Financial Model for Managing Return on Invested Capital (Step 1)

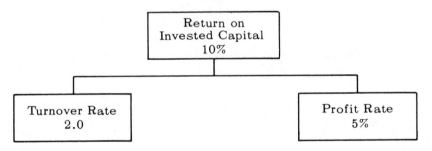

In selecting the combination of the turnover rate and the profit rate required to yield a 10 percent return on capital, consideration would be given first to the normal or average ratios for the particular industry since these would establish the overall benchmarks or probable operating parameters within which operations might be carried out. Then these two factors would be compared with current performance to determine whether they appeared to be attainable goals for the company. Once accepted as target rates, they would then be managed *together,* with the understanding that failure to meet the 5 percent profit rate, for example, would automatically dictate a need for a higher turnover of invested capital—or that a turnover rate of less than 2 must be compensated for by an increase in the rate of net earnings on sales.

The plan for operating control would then proceed to break down these overall standards into individual rates for each of the major elements to be managed, identifying the relative position of the next layer of subgoals or subobjectives. This next step, as shown in Exhibit 8, would thus translate the goal for the turnover of capital into a goal for the turnover of assets and would adjust the goal for a rate of profit after taxes to a pretax requirement expressed as a percentage of the sales dollar.

Exhibit 8

Financial Model for Managing Return on Invested Capital (Step 2)

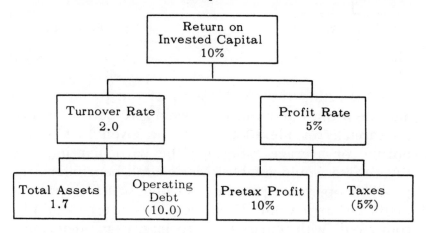

The goal for a turnover of 2 on total invested capital would now be managed through a combination of a 1.7

times turnover of total *assets* employed and a ratio of sales to operating debt of 10:1. This is expressed mathematically as a negative turnover rate since the operating debt represents that portion of the total assets not furnished by the invested capital of the company. The management of these two rates will also become interdependent since a decrease in accounts payable, for example, relative to sales income will increase the negative turnover rate for operating debt and place a demand for a higher positive turnover rate on the level of assets employed. If, on the other hand, greater use can be made of operating debt by taking full advantage of payment terms and thereby increasing the percentage of total assets supplied by trade creditors, a slower turnover of the total asset investment could be accepted and still meet the targeted rate of a 2 times turnover on capital. These two standards, in turn, will also be affected by a change in the rate of pretax earnings on sales—targeted at 10 percent on the assumption of a 50 percent rate of federal taxes on income—or by a change in the tax rate itself since this would affect the pretax profit rate required to maintain a constant rate of return on invested capital.

If these four subobjectives (as shown in Exhibit 8) appeared to be realistic as multiples required to reach the objective rate of return on capital, the model would then be expanded to describe the standards for each of the subelements of the asset structure and for each of the specific operating elements which would make up the pretax rate of a 10 percent return on sales. The turnover of total assets, for example, would normally be broken down into five major subgroupings, with three of these in turn divided into separate goals by profit

Exhibit 9

Financial Model for Managing Return on Invested Capital
(Step 3)

Asset Turnover 1.7

Cash 40.0 | Accounts Receivable 8.0 | Inventory 5.7 | Plant and Equipment 5.0 | Other Assets 13.3

Raw Material 25.0 | In-Process 25.0 | Finished 10.5

Product Line A 10.0 | Product Line B 4.0 | Nonassignable 4.0

center, by division, or by product line depending upon the particular structure of the business. Based on a 1.7 times turnover for total assets employed, typical values for the individual asset elements in a manufacturing business might appear as shown in Exhibit 9.

Dollar Allowances

On a planned sales volume base of $100,000, the targeted turnover rates developed at this point would result in the dollar allowances shown in Exhibit 10 for each element of asset investment.

Exhibit 10

Dollar Allowances for Each Element of Asset Investment

Asset	Turn-over	Total	Product A	Product B	Common
Cash	40.0	$ 2,500	—	—	$ 2,500
Accounts					
Receivable	8.0	12,500	$ 5,000	$ 7,000	500
Inventory:					
Raw Materials	25.0	4,000	500	1,500	2,000
In-Process	25.0	4,000	500	1,500	2,000
Finished	10.5	9,500	2,000	7,500	—
Total Inventory	5.7	17,500	3,000	10,500	4,000
Plant and					
Equipment	5.0	20,000	2,000	7,500	10,500
Other Assets	13.3	7,500	—	—	7,500
Total Assets	1.7	$60,000	$10,000	$25,000	$25,000
Turnover Rate	1.7	1.7	10.0	4.0	4.0

If each of the asset investments were then held exactly at the dollar level indicated by the planned turnover rates for each individual element, and if, in turn, the total dollar volume of sales were achieved at exactly $100,000 and at the sales mix as planned for product lines A and B, the composite result would be a turnover rate of 1.7 on total assets employed as targeted. Since actual performance, however, is seldom found to be 100 percent on plan in every single element of sales, sales mix, and level of investment in each individual asset account, the standards set for the individual turnover rates are not intended to portray the final actual results or even the separate levels of absolute control to be maintained. They are intended, instead, to provide a further set of working tools whereby anticipated changes can be foreseen and *balanced* against one another—an integrated plan for the management of assets that will indicate both the direction and the magnitude of change that must be accomplished if the overall rate of turnover is to be maintained.

Assume, for example, that the pretax profit rate of 10 percent on sales can be met and that no immediate change in the targeted turnover rate of 1.7 on total assets employed is thus required. The management of assets would then become the task of controlling the planned turnover rate on total investment or holding the level of assets at no more than $60,000 on a sales volume of $100,000. If it were then found that a planned change in the terms and conditions of sales indicated a slowdown in the turnover of investment in accounts receivable from the planned rate of 8 to a projected actual of 6, the resulting increase of some $4,000 in this asset account would have to be offset by a corresponding decrease in cash, inventory, plant and equipment, or the other-assets account.

In such a situation, each of these asset accounts would be checked to see whether corrective action could be taken to reduce the investment without in turn jeopardizing the operating support on which the rate of profit on sales would depend. On a short-term basis, it might be possible that no effective reduction could be made in either the plant and equipment account or the intangible items grouped under the heading of "other assets." This would then narrow down the areas of possible corrective action to a reduction in the cash account or a reduction in inventory.

Here, in turn, it might be found that the turnover of cash had already been maintained at the planned rate of 40, and that the cash balance of $2,500 could not be further reduced if the operating needs were to be met. This would leave the inventory account as the sole remaining possibility for a $4,000 reduction to offset the lower turnover of accounts receivable. Assume again that ways could be found to reduce the total inventory investment by a maximum of $2,000 without risking the sales and production plans. This would leave the total asset investment a net of $2,000 above plan for a turnover rate of only 1.6 versus the rate of 1.7 required as part of the plan to achieve a 10 percent rate of return on invested capital. This, in turn, would dictate a need for raising the profit rate from a pretax level of 10 percent to 10.6 percent of sales if the targeted rate of return on total assets is to be reached as part of the goal for return on capital employed. This balancing of turnover against profit then leads to an analysis of the individual operating factors which control the rate of profit on sales.

Analysis of Operating Elements

Although shown as a separate step in order to first describe the interaction and balancing required among the individual turnover rates established for each of the asset accounts, the analysis of the operating elements required to manage the profit rate is by no means secondary. In fact, it would actually be developed in parallel with the analysis of assets in establishing an overall plan for the balanced financial control of operations. In proceeding with the same basic objective of an assumed 10 percent rate of return on invested capital, the first two subelements or operating functions which would govern the required profit rate of a pretax 10 percent return on sales would be the elements of total income and total cost, elements which would appear in the financial model as shown in Exhibit 11.

These two elements will obviously determine the amount and the rate of pretax profits from operations. Yet they are not, in themselves, useful points of control

Exhibit 11

Financial Model for Managing Return on Invested Capital
(Step 4)

and can provide only the starting point for the development of the individual ratios which must be controlled and balanced. Gross sales are assumed, in this case, to provide the total income for the company. Sales volume must therefore be controlled at the planned dollar level of income if the programmed costs are to equal no more than 90 percent of sales, or, conversely, costs must be susceptible of downward adjustment if they are to be maintained in this model at a maximum of 90 percent on a declining sales base. The interrelationship and interdependence of these two factors—together with their joint dependence on the management of the turnover rate for assets employed—can be visualized more clearly as the subelements are described and given operating standards as a part of the overall plan. The next layer of control elements for which individual standards and ratios must be developed would appear when the financial model (see Exhibit 12) was again expanded to include the primary factors which will govern the level of income and the level of expense.

Elements of Total Cost

The dollar volume of gross sales, the element contributing 100 percent of the total income, has now been further defined as dependent upon a plan to market a total of 100,000 units of production at an average price of $1 each. Total cost, on the other hand, has been broken down into the two principal categories by which cost behavior can be predicted and from which different techniques for control will be developed. If the group identified as direct costs has been properly defined and properly analyzed, it may now be assumed that this cat-

Exhibit 12

*Financial Model for Managing Return on Invested Capital
(Step 5)*

egory of costs will vary directly with the volume of goods
produced and the volume of goods sold, thus providing
a direct link between this element of cost and the management of physical volume.

If operating performance were on standard, these
costs would be expected to rise and fall automatically
with changes in volume or to change in predictable fashion with changes in the product mix. If performance
were not on standard, the required corrective action
would be indicated by the measurement of variances
from standard direct cost—variances which would serve
as a direct measure of operating efficiency and would
pinpoint the specific areas for corrective action. Such
corrective action might be indicated, for example, in the
areas of material utilization and labor efficiency in production or the rate of direct variable expenses incurred
on the marketing side. Period expenses, on the other

hand, while measured initially as a percentage of sales income, would now be assigned a planned dollar level of expenditure. Henceforth it would be measured and controlled against these budgeted amounts, with the percentage-to-sales ratios used only to indicate the magnitude of adjustment required from time to time in order to balance this level of cost against all other elements in the plan.

Further expansion and detailing of the financial model would next proceed according to the sequence by which the elements in the operating plan were controlled or became subordinate to one another. This would be done in the order of importance or priority in establishing ratios and budgets. Assuming that the plan for sales volume, for example, would thus dictate the probable level of costs required—a more normal approach than one in which a fixed plan for costs and

Exhibit 13

Financial Model for Managing Return on Invested Capital (Step 6)

expenses is allowed to limit the volume which could be
produced and sold—the model would next identify the
details of the sales plan by specifying the price and unit
volume planned for each product line. The analysis of
sales elements would thus again be expanded as shown
in Exhibit 13.

Planned Mix of Sales

The management of the profit rate has, at this point,
been clearly identified as the integrated management of
physical volume, price, and cost. While the management
of cost has so far been described only by general
categories, the management of volume and price has
now been completely delineated and shown to be based
on the following planned mix of sales:

Product Line	Unit Volume	Price	Gross Sales
A	40,000	$ .85	$ 34,000
B	60,000	1.10	66,000
Total	100,000	$1.00	$100,000

Investment turnover of 1.7 has now resulted in a
planned asset level of $60,000 in conjunction with a
sales volume plan of $100,000, and since allowable
period expenses will also be developed from this same
sales base, the management of sales volume is shown to
be, not unexpectedly, the key control factor in the
operating plan. It is not, however, a factor to be managed in isolation from the other elements of financial
control. Not only is sales management dependent upon

the other elements for support, but it must, in itself, provide not only the required level of gross income to accomplish the planned turnover rate of assets committed, but must also provide that total income *at the planned rate of profitability*. In sales management, this will mean a continual balancing of unit volume, unit price, and product mix. It will require this balancing because the measure of profitability will rest, not on the gross dollar volume generated, but on the price/cost relationship of that volume which will determine the level of *profit contribution* from sales. This control point brings together the operating elements of volume, price, and the direct variable costs of production and marketing.

This relationship leads to the further development of the direct cost elements in the model—elements which might be found to have the typical values shown in Exhibit 14.

Manageable Costs

It will be noted that direct variable costs will normally be found both in production and in marketing since they are defined as those costs which bear a linear relationship to volume. The direct costs of production in a typical manufacturing operation would normally include direct materials consumed, the direct labor of production, and a minor list of overhead accounts that vary directly with the level of volume produced. The principal items in this latter category are the labor-related or fringe-benefit accounts associated with direct labor. While these do not, as a group, vary directly with a change in payroll, they are best regarded as a subfunc-

Exhibit 14

Financial Model for Managing Return on Invested Capital
(Step 7)

tion of the labor account itself and should follow the primary classification for labor costs.

In addition to sales commissions, which are typically a direct variable percentage of the dollar volume of goods sold, the direct marketing costs also include a provision for the sales deductions group as a cost element. This differs from the usual accounting treatment given to such items as cash discount, transportation, returns and allowances, and policy adjustments—a group which is normally deducted from gross sales as a type of negative income and often omitted entirely from the usual financial statement which treats *net* sales as the starting point for profit control. Inclusion of the sales deductions group as a direct variable element of marketing cost recognizes these items as *manageable costs* and gives them a controllable value in a balanced financial plan.

Since each element of direct cost is associated with a unit of production or with a dollar of sales, each of the direct cost accounts can be further identified or subdivided into totals by product-line categories. In doing so, it will be noted that the product-line totals are expressed *as a percentage of total sales* in the model rather than shown as percentages of their respective portions of the planned volume.

Inasmuch as the use of the financial model in controlling the targeted rate of return on capital will depend on the ability to balance each of the operating elements as an integral part of the whole, this serves to identify the overall impact of each product or product line as a part of the total profit plan and to indicate the magnitude of change required in balancing one element against another.

Period Expense Budgets

With the need for direct costs established and identified as to rate and dollar amount required to produce
and market the volume of goods planned, the final sec-
tion of the operating plan—the development of period
expense budgets—will complete the matrix of the financial model. Although last in the sequence, the plan for
period expenses in support of operations is by no means
as simple a task as the mere arbitrary allocation of the
remaining funds available, and it cannot be determined
by the process of backing into the dollar limit indicated
by other elements of the plan.

Many of the period expenses will already have been
determined to a large extent by previous decisions—for
example, on the planned investment in assets. These
decisions will dictate the requirements for such time-
oriented expenses as insurance and local taxes on the
property accounts, handling and storage of inventories,
and depreciation of buildings and equipment. Other
decisions taken in the area of direct cost operations
for marketing and production will also create the need
for a series of such period overhead expenses as
maintenance, supervision, advertising, and administration.

These basic requirements may leave little room for
such indirect or nonrelated expenses as research and
development or general administration, and the total
need for period expense support may well exceed the
remaining cost allowance assigned by other requirements of the financial plan. The budgeting of period
expenses should, however, be based primarily on the
need for cost support rather than planned as a percent-

age of available income. The need must be developed first. If the total requirements are then found to exceed the mathematical limits of the model, the model itself will then be put to the very use for which it was designed—the process of adjusting and balancing the other control elements until a satisfactory plan for the total operation of the business has been developed in final form.

Assuming the 40 percent of sales indicated for supporting expenses to be sufficient in this example, the planning and budgeting of period expenses might next be developed by general categories with typical cost relationships as shown in Exhibit 15.

In developing the plan for period expenses, it will be noted that only a minor portion of such expenses are normally identified by product line, with only $15,000 or roughly one-third of the total supporting expenses of $40,000 shown as *assignable* product-line expenses in Exhibit 15.

This does not conform to the practice of overhead allocation as followed in accounting systems based on absorption costing and, in fact, avoids any attempts to allocate portions of those expenses which exist as *common overhead* or which are required to support the business as a whole. Instead, the assignable period expenses are defined as those in direct support of a particular product or product line and are categorized as overheads which would no longer exist if the product line itself were discontinued. On this basis, period expenses in the financial plan or model can be adjusted or balanced directly against individual changes made or proposed for the product-line elements of investment or in the direct cost of operations.

Exhibit 15

Financial Model for Managing Return on Invested Capital
(Step 8)

The Overall Plan for Business Control

With the plan for period expenses completed, the individual parts of the financial model would then be brought together into a final form which would consolidate the several sections for volume, cost, and investment, and which would then portray a complete and fully integrated plan for balanced financial control. In condensed form, omitting the subdivisions and ratios by product line, the overall plan for business control would appear as shown in Exhibit 16.

When completed, the operating model will not only provide a useful working tool to be used in the decision-making process but will portray in logical sequence each of the fundamental concepts of basic financial management itself:

- It will give primary emphasis to the cost of capital concept by starting with the overall objective for return on invested capital while establishing standards and objectives for each element of operations and investment.
- It will demonstrate the interrelationship of turnover and profit and the need for the simultaneous management of these two primary points of control.
- It will assign relative values to the management of assets by measuring investment and turnover as an integral part of total operations.
- It will describe the exact relationship of volume, price, and mix required in the management of sales.
- It will present an analysis of total cost in terms of cost behavior by element, providing immediate ac-

Exhibit 16

Financial Model for Managing Return on Invested Capital
(Overall Plan)

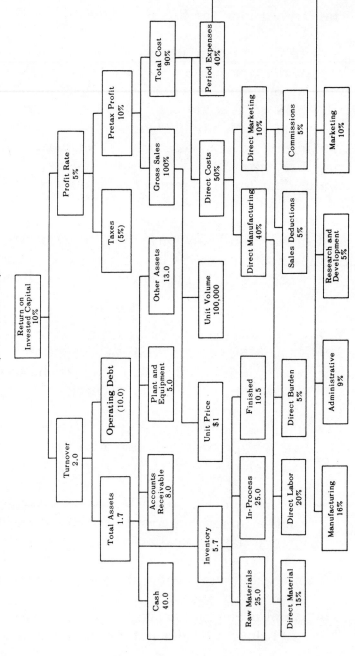

cess and visibility to areas for corrective action and effective control.

- It will provide, in total, a fully integrated plan for balanced financial control of all the elements which must be managed in the operation of a business.

In summary, the need for a complete perspective in business management requires a form of measurement and analysis which goes beyond the confines of traditional accounting procedure. It calls for changes in the appraisal of values and changes in the meaning of reported results. It calls, in short, for a new approach to financial reporting.

9

The Measurement
of Results

ACCOUNTING is often described as the language of
business because it deals with the elements of income
and expense and speaks in terms of profit and loss.
Thus it appears to identify itself directly with the basic
aims and objectives of the profit motive of business operations. If it is to speak for business, however, it must
do so in a manner which will (1) provide a comprehen-
sive analysis of results, (2) guide management toward
the proper objectives of financial control, and (3) measure accomplishment in concise and understandable
terms.

In brief, accounting must serve the needs of the
business rather than the needs of a system and, for
internal management control, must remain both flexible

and adaptable to the changing demands of information retrieval, information processing, and information reporting. Although each will play a substantial role in the development of a system for the financial measurement and control of operations, it is in the field of financial reporting that accounting will find its greatest usefulness—or will, in many cases, fail to meet the challenge altogether. Where it does fail to meet the needs of management, the accounting presentation of financial reports can often trace its inadequacy to its own origins and traditions, to practices followed for the sake of uniformity, or to concepts established to meet the needs of auditing procedures rather than the economic appraisal of results.

Financial Reports

Present-day financial reporting had its beginnings in the advent of double-entry bookkeeping, a system which produced an orderly flow of balanced accounts from the journals of original entry into the ledgers and from the ledgers into the casting up of accounts known as the trial balance. It was from this accounting summation that two separate and largely unrelated financial statements—the balance sheet and the profit and loss or income statement—were developed. Of the two, the balance sheet was clearly regarded as the senior statement, being described in early accounting literature as the "fundamental statement, the ultimate goal of double-entry bookkeeping."

Conceived in its present form long before the current widespread public ownership of the industrial enterprise, the balance sheet served chiefly as a source of credit information through its presentation of assets in the order of liquidity and through its segregation of the capital structure into the apparently unrelated elements of debt and equity. The income statement of profit and loss came into being at a later date purely as an appendage, or supplement, to the balance sheet and was immediately assigned a secondary role as "primarily reflecting and accounting for the change in the equity as a result of operations . . . a sort of connecting link between undistributed earnings at the beginning and at the end of a fiscal period."

In essence, these two financial reports were designed as little more than a summation of the bookkeeping procedures or a rearrangement of the trial balance. As accounting statements, they have remained virtually unchanged for more than a century—a period which has witnessed the almost complete reversal of their original roles, with the profit and loss statement gradually emerging as the senior or dominant document. Unfortunately, in spite of the increasing usefulness of operations accounting in providing functional classifications of income and expense categories and in using ratios and percentages, the increasing dominance of the profit and loss statement did not, of itself, serve to integrate the two reports. Instead, by relegating the balance sheet to a position of apparent secondary importance, it gave continued emphasis to the original impression of separation and segregation. This lack of any attempt at integrated financial reporting is evident in the definitions assigned to these two reports. The income statement clearly is defined as a report intended to show the results of operations for a period of time, as opposed to the statement of condition at a given moment in time as presented by the balance sheet.

Obsolescence of Accounting Statements

These seemingly diverse attributes have not only gone unchanged; they have gone unchallenged and, in fact, have actually solidified their position over the years through repeated adherence to established form and custom. Such financial reports are obsolete, not simply because they have remained unchanged, but, more importantly, because they no longer meet the requirements of modern business management. Evidence of this obsolescence is abundant, with the strongest indictments supplied by those charged with the responsibility for taking action: the operating managers themselves. To these managers, the inadequacy of the traditional profit and loss statement as an effective management tool has long been apparent. When it came to the point of analyzing and interpreting the details of operations, modern managers have for some time found it necessary to abandon the customary bookkeeping presentations still found in the certified accounting statements and to supplant these with reports which have introduced new concepts and new measurements. For internal reports this began with the use of budgets and standard costs, a step which substituted for the first time *a statement of what costs should have been* for the purely historical summary of costs actually incurred or accounted for during the fiscal period.

Management then found statistical data desirable in its reporting of sales revenues, its measuring of performance against existing markets, and its analyzing of sales income by product and by sales region. More recently, it has found traditional cost accounting concepts inadequate and has moved into the use of direct costing, a major departure from the trial balance school of accounting statements. These and similar changes in the internal structure of the income statement all indicated a basic need for a means of measuring and evaluating certain factors which were not provided directly from the books of account. They did not, however, constitute any substantive change in the fundamental nature of financial reporting since even the revised statements of income and expense were still only distantly related to the information presented in the balance sheet, with as yet no indication that the two might have any direct bearing on each other.

The Integration of Profit and Capital

It was not until the continued growth of industrial activity brought greater and greater demands for increasing amounts of new capital investment that the first tentative steps were taken to formally link the elements of profit and capital into one unified report. This began with the need to measure the projected return on proposed new capital investment, a basic measurement which had until then been isolated from the routine financial reports as being of statistical value only. These attempts to evaluate the return on new investment led, quite naturally, to an appraisal of the return on existing investment, a technique which has since been expanded to the measurement of divisional, plant, and individual product-line operations.

Important as this was in establishing an initial breakthrough in the coupling of profits and capital in a formal financial report, it fell short of supplying a definitive or truly quantitative result, even within the confines of strictly internal reports. Where used, the reference to return on investment became a relative term which merely conveyed the idea of *degrees of profitability.* This carried with it the strong implication that any return, however modest, represented an economic gain for the business and that the higher rates of return simply indicated a further enrichment or accumulation of wealth for the benefit of the stockholder. Seldom did the reporting techniques take the final and logical step of measuring *the return on total capital employed* or state, in absolute terms, the profit requirement generated by the size of the capital structure which had been created to support the level of operations. To all intents and purposes, the forward progress of financial reporting came to a halt at this point, leaving the basic elements of capital and profit still fragmented and dispersed.

The seeming indifference to the fundamental relationship which exists between profit and capital stems in large part from accounting definitions and usages which have gained widespread recognition and acceptance in the name of uniformity. It is, in fact, one of the tenets of uniform accounting principles that has so erroneously defined the term "profit" as *"the excess of income over expense,"* with the word "expense" in turn narrowly defined as representing the aggregate of those costs and expenses flowing through the books of account, whether actually paid or charged against income for the period by means of amortization or accrual. In this context, the term "profit" has been given a *remainder value* as the simple algebraic sum of the bookkeeping debits and credits to the operating accounts, an arithmetic plus or minus to be determined from the periodic casting up of the accounts, an amount denoting the final overall results from operations and therefore requiring no further analysis or appraisal.

The Missing Element

It is indeed surprising that the practice of accounting—so meticulous in its insistence on matching related items of income and expense for a fiscal period—should be content with a system which continues to ignore one significant element of cost, an element not only substantial in magnitude but basic to the very concept of economic profit itself. The missing element is, of course, the cost of capital employed in the business. It is missing, apparently, simply because it does not exist in the form of an invoice to be entered and paid or because there is no accounting or bookkeeping procedure whereby such a cost may be amortized or accrued on the regular books of account. Thus ignored in this area, it exists—where it is recognized at all—somewhat as an abstract term, an undefined value not related to the double-entry concept which produces the balance sheet and its companion statement of profit and loss.

While true in total, this statement is, curiously enough, *not true with respect to the cost of borrowed capital.* The interest charges on debt capital are definitive, represent known and exact amounts, and occur with predictable regularity over stated periods of time. They are therefore accorded normal accounting recognition in the income statement and are included in the group of costs and expenses deemed to be a proper charge against income for the period. It is quite possibly this very distinction in accounting treatment—the bookkeeping recognition of the cost of only the debt portion of the capital structure—which has led to the oft-stated assumption on the part of so many business managers that *equity capital has, in fact, no cost!*

That this belief actually prevails in some quarters is evident in the myriad mistaken decisions involving capital outlays for expansion, for new plant and equipment, or for proposed increases in the working-capital elements of inventory and accounts receivable. If additional debt is to be the source of such new capital, such decisions are not infrequently made by comparing the projected rate of return on investment with the interest cost of money. If the funds can be borrowed at 6 percent interest, so the reasoning goes, a calculated return at a safe 7 or 8 percent on the new venture will yield more than the cost of interest and will therefore be "profitable." Since the total cost of capital is not an integral part of the financial reporting structure, it is often ignored or perhaps not even recognized in the decision-making process.

A New Concept of Profit

A new concept of profit is needed, one which will assign to the term an economic value—a value directly related to the cost and the risk of the capital employed. The need for this concept of profit, as well as the fallacy of present accounting practice, can best be illustrated by comparing the typical financial reports of two companies that are exactly alike in every respect except one—the makeup of their capital structure. Such a comparison is shown in Exhibit 17.

There are several inferences which would normally be drawn from statements of this type.

- In summary form, the stockholders or potential investors will be informed that Company A earned

Exhibit 17

A Comparison of Accounted Financial Reports

Profit and Loss Statement	Company A	Company B
Sales	$2,000,000	$2,000,000
Direct Cost of Goods Sold	1,000,000	1,000,000
Marginal Contribution	1,000,000	1,000,000
Period Expenses:		
Operations	830,000	830,000
Interest Expense	10,000	82,000
Total Period Expense	$ 840,000	$ 912,000
Pretax Profit	$ 160,000	$ 88,000
Net Earnings	$ 80,000	$ 44,000
Earnings per Share	$1.00	$2.20
Capital Employed		
First Mortgate Note		
@ 5%	$ 200,000	$ 200,000
Debentures @ 6%	—	200,000
Subordinated Debentures		
@ 15%	—	400,000
Common Stock		
@ $10 Par	800,000	200,000
Total Capital Employed	$1,000,000	$1,000,000

only $1 per share for the period, while Company B reported a much higher level of earnings, $2.20 a share.

- In some quarters, these reported per-share earnings might then be evaluated at a price/earnings ratio to determine the market value of the common stock. If the prevailing price/earnings ratio were, for example, 15:1, it is not altogether unlikely that some "investors" might attribute a value of $15 a share to the stock of Company A, while placing a price of $33 a share on the higher reported per-share earnings of Company B, even though operating performance of the two companies is identical.

- The management of Company B, also using earnings per share as its sole criterion, might easily be persuaded that still more debt—if indeed it could be obtained—would provide a desirable increase in "leverage" for the common equity while at the same time making decisions for new capital outlays on the basis of a return above the cost of interest.

The obvious fallacies in this reasoning are ones which present accounting and financial reporting practice do little or nothing to dispel, but rather appear to foster or actually encourage by the hybrid use of the term "profit" and by repeated emphasis on the statistical measurement of earnings per share. The fallacy exists, first of all, *in charging only a portion of the cost of capital* against current income. By giving recognition to the cost of debt capital as interest expense and by remaining silent on the cost of equity capital, accounting theory and financial practice alike give the unmistakable impression that equity capital has no cost. What is more, use of the earnings-per-share measure gives strong support to the leverage theory of financial management. This says, in effect, that (1) the earnings on borrowed capital need only be sufficient to cover the interest cost and that (2) since all remaining profits accrue to the benefit of the common equity, a steady gain in per-share earnings is a desirable business goal unto itself, regardless of the level of debt financing. By this process, not only is *total capital employed* fragmented into apparently unrelated elements in the reporting format, but the *total cost of capital*, one of the major operating costs of the business, is omitted in the determination of profit.

A New Approach to Financial Reporting

A full understanding of the fundamental need for evaluating return on capital *as the primary financial measurement* should dictate a new approach to financial reporting, providing a new type of financial statement, a statement which will bridge the gap between bookkeeping and financial analysis and between the trial balance type of reporting and the need for management planning and control. The new report should be a marriage of the present balance sheet and income statement concepts, a final bringing-together of the bilateral elements of profit and capital in a form which will give recognition to their mutual interdependence. Not only should such a report identify the total cost of total capital employed, but it should put the measurement of profit into proper focus *as an economic gain or loss* in place of the present remainder value assigned to it by mere bookkeeping procedures. A report which would embody these concepts and accomplish these aims might well take the form of the report presented in Exhibit 18.

A report of this type would serve several purposes:

- It would segregate and highlight the amount of pretax margin from operations, a figure which usually must be extracted from the body of reports as they are now published. This would free the year-by-year or company-by-company comparisons of current operating results from the interest cost effect of differences in capital structures.
- It would maintain the identity of the traditional net-income or net-profit-after-taxes figure, but would assign to it a new value as simply the *increase in book equity,* a description intended to distinguish

Exhibit 18

Integrated Financial Report

	Company A	Company B
Sales	$2,000,000	$2,000,000
Direct Cost of Goods Sold	1,000,000	$1,000,000
Marginal Contribution	1,000,000	1,000,000
Operating Period Expenses	830,000	830,000
Pretax Operating Margin	170,000	170,000
Interest on Borrowed Capital	10,000	82,000
Taxable Income	160,000	88,000
Federal Taxes on Income	80,000	44,000
Increase in Book Equity	80,000	44,000
Add—Net Interest Cost	5,000	41,000
Net Return on Total Capital	85,000	85,000
Cost of Capital Employed @ 10%	100,000	100,000
Economic Gain (Loss)	$ (15,000)	$ (15,000)

this increment from the concept of economic profit.

- By adding back the net after-tax cost of the interest on borrowed capital, the new report would also provide a clear statement of *total earnings on total capital,* a step which divorces the previous accounted results from the effects of changes in the capital structure itself. In the examples given for Company A and Company B, this step would eliminate one major weakness currently imposed on financial reporting by the limitations of present accounting practice: the fact that, in reporting net income for Company B, *a substantial portion of the cost of capital has already been charged against operations for the period* in the form of interest expense. At the same time, Company A seemingly enjoys a much larger "profit" simply because the greater part of its cost of capital has not yet been taken into account.

- Finally, by placing a quantitative measure on the cost of capital employed, the true economic gain or loss for the business enterprise can be shown in dollars and cents for the first time. Once the impact of this final value has been fully absorbed and understood, it should provide the investor with a better evaluation of the earning power of the capital he has put out at risk; perhaps more importantly, it should provide the manager who is charged with the profitable employment of that capital a measurable and more meaningful standard of operating performance.

The difficulties in carrying out such a change in financial reporting will be found, not primarily in resistance to the basic concept that all capital has a cost, but in attempts to arrive at a precise measurement of that cost, a common denominator which can be universally applied and accepted. While it may be generally accepted that a minimum 10 percent cost of capital is a reasonable approximation for the average industrial concern when compared with the smaller degree of risk inherent in the regulated operations of the public utilities, there is admittedly no immediate short-term measurement comparable to the simple calculation of interest cost on borrowed money which can be readily applied to determine the exact cost of total capital employed. This difficulty, however, should not be allowed to stand in the way of adopting such a report, any more than the difficulty of determining the exact life of a depreciable asset has stood in the way of charging the cost of depreciation against presently reported values for accounted profit.

In the final analysis, the basic financial management of a successful business operation will depend on the integrated management of capital and profit. The measurement of that relationship will therefore become a fundamental and vital part of the periodic appraisal of results.

10

Accounting for Inflation

PROFIT management—with or without inflation—has always been dependent to a large extent on what the accounting process provides in the way of profit measurement. And since this dependence on accounting principles, accounting procedures, and accounting measurements is likely to continue for some time to come, the concepts and methods of the accounting process form a very basic foundation for the management of profit itself.

Accounting has until recently been a highly structured profession with both rigid definitions and strictly prescribed procedures. With both form and content dating well back into the last century, the process has leaned heavily on what has been thought of as conservatism, an approach which has produced a narrow view of the values assigned to the balance sheet as well as a technician's view of the measurement of profit itself. This parochial attitude has not fared well under the changing needs of the business enterprise, and indeed the accounting profession has shown considerable reluctance to deal with the evolving complexities of tax legislation as well as the continuing erosion of monetary values. Its code of *uniform accounting principles* has, in fact, become a shambles of differing opinions, a rapid deterioration of professional expertise that has brought with it seemingly endless confusion and litigation, factors which have served to severely discredit both the worth and the credibility of the accounting process and accounting measurements. The inadequacies of the past have been a source of mounting frustration to management and the investor alike, but have perhaps at least held the promise of eventual solution under normal economic conditions. With the advent of continuing inflation, however, that promise is no longer apparent and the time needed for corrective action no longer available.

Inflation has placed a burden on the accounting process which now makes immediate change not only desirable, but mandatory. Where previous weaknesses were perhaps tolerable for a period of time in that they might eventually sort themselves out in a revision of principles responding to an evolving need, the time for such gradual correction is now past and the opportunity for piecemeal adjustment lost. Inflation has imposed a whole new set of conditions, conditions which cannot be met by the slow process of revision but which strike at the very concepts on which the entire process of accounting has been built. The need for drastic and substantive change not only has become readily apparent, but has found a considerable voice in the financial press, a voice coming from many directions at once and echoing a common theme.

Numerous articles and editorials have dealt with the problem of the massive overstatement of profits stemming from inadequate methods of inventory accounting as well as from the undercosting of charges based solely on original-cost depreciation. The impact of these two forces on the rapid erosion of business capital is well documented, as is the resulting diversion of earnings to the tax collector—a diversion of cash flow away from replacement needs in the form of a tax on capital itself.

What is not as well documented or apparently as well understood is the consequent undervaluation of capital and assets employed, an undervaluation that has equally devastating effects on future profits, both in the level of profit goals and measurements as well as in the more immediate needs for a pricing base.

The need for change in the accounting process is thus seen from many directions at once, a need backed up by convincing evidence of confusion and distortion in the reporting of profits when based on the concepts of present accounting procedures and methods. The few solutions suggested, however, are far from adequate and are not likely to work, not if the previous record of adaptability to change on the part of the accounting profession is any indication of a probable response to the problem. Accounting, as a profession, has not only been slow to change in the past, but has shown a peculiar affinity for clinging to the past.

In recent years, for example, the profession has been a notable opponent of the use of direct costing, opposing it on the academic ground of not being consistent with generally accepted accounting principles. This argument could effectively serve to rule out any and all changes in method on the basis that change itself did not conform to the past. In spite of this occasional myopic view toward progress in the use of accounting, not only has direct costing survived but its use is continually expanding throughout business due to the simple fact that *it meets a need for better reporting and for better management.*

This same attitude of resistance also prevailed briefly during the early years of computerized accounting when reluctance was evident in the process of transferring the general ledger accounts from handwritten records to magnetic tape. The computers won, but only by the sheer impact of technology and economics, not because of any ready desire on the part of the accounting profession to accept change.

Such resistance to change has had substantial impact in many areas of financial management, but perhaps the greatest effect of the historical accounting process has been in its technical definition of profit and in the strong influence this definition has had on the profit management of business.

Profit, in the accounting sense, has been defined as the net remainder value shown on the operating statement—the *bottom-line* measurement which suggests a final evaluation of net earnings after all costs and expenses have been duly accounted for. And in accepting this measurement and definition of profit, business has gauged its progress accordingly and has based its future goals and objectives for earnings on the same kind of *profit* measurement. It is not, however, a measurement of profit in any economic sense of the word since it typically records no more than a partial or hybrid measurement of results, much less a statement of results in terms of current value.

The accounting measurement of profit is a hybrid measurement for the simple reason that it reports neither the total earnings from operations nor the total earnings on capital employed, but a mixture of the two. Following *generally accepted accounting principles,* the income statement includes all the operating costs of materials, labor, and overhead expenses—as would be expected—but then proceeds to add only one portion of the fourth element of cost, the cost of capital employed. It does this by accounting for interest expense on debt capital as a charge against operations, since the charge for interest is both tax deductible and readily measureable, and by then defining the net amount remaining on the bottom line as *profit.* The resulting measurement is not only meaningless in itself, but since the answer is an incomplete one, it forces the user of the statement to reconstruct the full measurement of earnings, to finish the job which the accounting process has left hanging in midair. It forces the users of the statement—both management and the analyst—to complete the job in one of two ways, either to add back the net interest cost to the accounted earnings in order to find the total stream of operating earnings to be measured as a rate of return against the total capital employed, or to go in the opposite direction and to also include the missing portion of the cost of capital as a further charge against operations for the period. The missing portion is, of course, the cost of equity capital, by far the larger of the two cost of capital elements.

The accounting definition of profit must be changed by one method or the other, and of the two the concept of charging the cost of equity capital against income as a cost element offers a more substantive approach to profit measurement, and with it the opportunity for a more thorough understanding of the need to recover all the costs of doing business as a basic premise for profit management.

This latter move has been strongly endorsed by Robert Anthony of the Harvard Business School, whose article "Accounting for the Cost of Equity" stated that the "use of equity capital has a cost, undeniably, although accountants do not record it; business would be far better off if they did." Professor Anthony argues convincingly that "accounting should adopt the economics concept of interest—that is, regular accounting procedures should take cognizance of the cost of using equity capital."

The accounting process, then, is seen as a less than adequate tool for profit measurement—and hence for profit management—even under what might be described as normal economic conditions. And when this same process is projected into an economy of rapidly rising inflation it is hopelessly outdated and totally inadequate. It requires basic change in both concept and method in at least three fundamental areas.

Balance Sheet Accounting

Inflation attacks the balance sheet much more subtly than the way in which it obviously affects the operating accounts. While underdepreciation of equipment and FIFO inventory valuations result in highly distorted and inflated reports of earnings, the effect on the valuation of assets and capital is not so readily discernible and by no means as quickly apparent. In fact, inflation has perhaps its greatest impact *on the erosion of capital itself.*

In considering the assets of a business provided by the use of capital, it is perhaps fair to state that inflation has little impact on such assets as cash or receivables, assets that not only are quite current in nature but tend to ride with inflation in the sense that they represent essentially current values at any point in time.

The true impact of inflation on the balance sheet first surfaces with the inventory accounts, where the present choice of an accounting method often tends to minimize one problem while creating another. Where the LIFO method of inventory valuation is used—a method of charging the most recent (and inflated) costs against current income—the inflationary effect of inventory profit is removed from the operating statement while the earlier and lower costs are left in the inventory account, a process which leaves the asset value considerably understated on the balance sheet in terms of current replacement value. In similar fashion, the opposite method of FIFO inventory valuation—the first-in, first-out method of accounting—leaves the more recent and inflated acquisition costs in the inventory while frequently recording a substantial inventory profit on the operating statement. Other methods such as average costing and standard costing of the inventory merely serve to avoid both extremes in a compromise which then weakens the reported values on both financial statements at the same time.

It is thus obvious that no single method of inventory valuation currently provided by normal accounting standards can withstand the effects of inflation. Nor is it sufficient to reason that, since inventory is constantly being renewed through the process of acquisition and sale, the asset will tend to adjust to inflated values over the longer term as new inventory replaces the old.

A new method of inventory valuation is needed to meet the new conditions imposed by inflation, a method which will simultaneously meet the needs of income statement and balance sheet alike. And since recorded costs, under inflation, are obsolete almost as soon as they are entered on the books, the need is clearly to *value inventories at anticipated levels of cost,* costs which will reflect replacement values at least over the near term. Such a method has already found a need, with some managements describing it as the NIFO or next-in, first-out method of accounting. In concept, it will appear to run contrary to those generally accepted accounting principles which have clung to the dictum that inventories must at all times be stated *at the lower of cost or market,* a standard which may appeal to the sense of conservatism but which has little else to recommend it. In the final analysis, the dispute need not be with the wording of the method at all but could be resolved with a simple redefinition of the word *cost.* In current usage the cost value of inventory is considered to be the original acquisition cost, a value which has little relevance in an inflationary spiral. Cost must be restated in terms of replacement cost, not only for inventories but as a concept that will move the entire historical accounting process forward into a system of current value accounting.

A second and by far more serious impact of inflation on the balance sheet will be found to exist in the so-called fixed asset accounts for land, buildings, machinery, and equipment—assets which will typically not be renewed or replaced as rapidly as inventory and whose stated value will very quickly become obsolete under rising rates of inflation. The problem here centers around what has already been called the "accounting profession's increasingly illogical attachment to original-cost depreciation."

This concept, with the exception of values shown for land, not only records the cost at the date of acquisition—a cost which no longer bears any resemblance to current replacement value—but then proceeds to write such cost down by means of depreciation charges at the same time that inflation is driving the cost of replacing the asset sharply upward. The accounting process thus drives a widening wedge between depreciated acquisition cost and current value, a process which in a short span of time severely understates the economic value of assets employed. This divergence of values has obvious impact on the operating statement, where the overstatement of earnings resulting from inadequate charges for depreciation will immediately result in higher income taxes on the inflated earnings, taxes which are in effect a tax on capital itself. The end result is that the overstatement of earnings has effectively diverted to the tax collector the cash needed to replace such assets, an erosion of capital which can only accelerate as inflation continues.

Nor is the problem of fixed asset valuation by any means confined to those assets which a company owns and which are at least recorded on the balance sheet. A larger problem, and a growing one for many companies, exists in the accounting treatment given to leased assets. The concept of capitalizing lease obligations in terms of present worth may satisfy the statement of liabilities on the right-hand side of the balance sheet, but it falls far short of the need on the left-hand side to reflect the true value of the assets required to run the business.

Such a point of view seems to suggest that assets and capital have economic value only when they are in fact owned by the business and not because they may in fact be generating the bulk of the earnings.

Leasing, in any form, is clearly a use of debt capital, a source which provides the assets of business as surely and as directly as any other form of capital. It must be recognized as such, and the niceties of present accounting distinctions must be submerged in favor of a reporting system that recognizes not only the total values employed in a business but also the need to state such values in terms of current economic worth—in other words, the cost in present dollars to replace existing facilities using current technology with those of a comparable productive capacity.

Operations Accounting

While the need for change in accounting procedures on the balance sheet is one of reporting the current value of all assets employed in the business, the need for change on the income statement goes beyond the impact of depreciation charges and the costing of inventory against shipments. Inflation is also impacting directly on many of the operating accounts whose charges do not originate with the asset valuation on the balance sheet but flow directly into the operating stream. These charges which do not flow through the asset accounts will be found in many of the major elements of period expense or fixed overhead—charges which are expensed directly as incurred against income for the period. And to the extent that such charges are also inadequate, profits will again be overstated and available cash diverted to pay higher taxes rather than held to meet the needs of rising costs.

In many industries, the rising cost of labor in the form of salaries and wages may well be the area of greatest concern. Current wage levels are by no means standing still but are on an upward curve that appears to be irreversible as long as inflation continues. And not only are higher wage demands thus quite predictable; in many cases they have already been agreed to under various types of labor contracts. In either case, it makes little sense to account for labor costs which are either obsolescent or already obsolete and to wait until pending events actually take place before giving them recognition in the financial statement of operations. It has been said that the military is always well prepared for the last war, and the sad reality is that business is also well prepared for the past when it bases its measurements and judgments on the accounted results of events which are not likely to occur again.

The same reasoning will also hold true—although possibly to a lesser degree—in many other overhead accounts such as supplies, utilities, maintenance, and travel. Again, the cost spiral is either predictable or already announced, giving a clear indication of the probable new levels of cost about to be incurred. Here, the present posture of accounting seems to be one of compromise and indecision. Present practice does allow for the accrual of costs and expenses, in advance of their actual occurrence, but only to the extent that such costs represent a known or measurable quantity at the time the accounting is rendered. This policy also contains a certain amount of flexibility with respect to probable future costs and losses. The flexibility may be based on experience ratios as in providing for anticipated losses

on uncollectable accounts, or it may be based on projected costs arising from a management decision to close
down or abandon certain of its operating facilities.

A more positive tone is needed, a broadening of the
accounting concept of costs and expenses to include not
only those costs already incurred, but those which are
about to take place. And while such a change must
clearly be tempered with reasonable judgment both by
management and by the accountant who will attest to
the results, the need for judgment is certainly no
stranger to the accounting process, and the use of reasonable approximations no departure from present
practice. The accounting change, if it can be brought
about, might also serve to pave the way for more en-
lightened tax legislation which would alleviate the present inequities of tax confiscation under inflation. Until
then, management will have an urgent need to set its
own accounting standards if accounted operations are
to reflect the proper management of profit.

Profit Accounting

Once the basic accounting process has been changed
to reflect current values of all assets employed on the
balance sheet and to reflect a statement of replacement
costs in the operating results, the stage will be set for the
proper measurement of profit. And if profit is indeed to
be managed under inflation, the need for a proper measurement and evaluation of profit will be paramount.

The first responsibility of the accounting profession
in this vital area of reporting is to abandon its tacit support and approval of many of the partial and pseudo
profit measurements presently in use. Foremost among

these should be a move to completely discard the Earnings-per-Share report as any more than a vehicle to be used in the price/earnings multiple. Its wide use throughout industry has been highly misleading in the past, to management and the investor alike, and its continued use under inflation can be no less than disastrous. Since it is not related to any base of investment dollars, but simply to the number of shares of common equity outstanding, it not only will serve to support a picture of inflated earnings but will effectively mask the continuing erosion of capital.

Second, and to a somewhat lesser degree, the measurement of accounted profit as a percentage Return on Equity—where used—must be put into proper perspective and the effect of debt leverage clearly set forth. Although high rates of Return on Equity have generally been discredited in the past when they were plainly achieved through high leverage or excessive use of debt—a capital structure which obviously imposed added risk on the equity investment and hence called for a substantially higher rate of return to justify the higher risk—the extremes to which this measurement has been put have been confined to a small minority of companies up until the present time. Under inflation, however, the extremes can quickly become the norm, with the Return-on-Equity measurement of profit rapidly becoming as misleading a tool as Earnings per Share. Inflation is making capital a scarce commodity at the same time that business is experiencing a growing need for additional capital to finance that same inflation. And with inflation, the deterioration in the quality of earnings does little to attract new equity capital.

These factors combine to drive business more heavily into the use of debt capital, to a greater use of leverage than many companies have been accustomed to in the past. And assuming that the use of additional debt capital returns something more than the interest cost it creates, the leverage of apparent results as measured by Return on Equity may be substantial indeed. This compression of earnings against a shrinking equity base will have little to do with profitability or with profit management since any reported increase in the rates of return will be no more than added compensation for added risk.

Third, profits measured in terms of the rate of Return on Sales—a measurement not even remotely connected to any form of investment—will have even less meaning than before since the use of added capital required to finance the inflated level of sales would remain totally unaccounted for.

These and other forms of the partial measurement of profit may well become the victims of inflation through the sheer weight of necessity. The accounting profession, however, has not only the opportunity but the responsibility to take leadership in profit accounting at a time when a clear understanding and a valid measurement of economic profit are needed most. This will inevitably narrow down to the measurement of Return on Invested Capital, a measurement which not only must be based on the total of all capital actually employed but with all elements fully measured under a system of current value accounting.

11

Reducing the Cost
of Inflation

THE management of profit under inflation will, as has
been seen, first depend upon a system of accounting
that measures results in terms of current economic
value in place of a system of recorded historical costs.
Once this step has been accomplished, and the necessary
tools for profit measurement fully developed, attention
must turn to the question of how to manage a business
profitably under an economy of eroding values.

The first and most obvious inclination is to raise
prices to offset the rising cost of operations, and perhaps
to keep on raising prices as frequently as costs go up. It
is also obvious, however, that the marketplace will
sooner or later set a limit on price increases—even
under spiraling inflation—and that attempts to manage

profits through price alone must eventually reach a point of diminishing returns. Other avenues are indeed open and in fact have been open in many companies for some time, avenues for the improved management of profit which have for the most part been neglected because there was no pressing need, no sense of urgency to take corrective action. And inflation, for all its ills, may indeed succeed—where more leisurely events have failed—in eventually forcing action where action should have been taken earlier in the better management of profit.

While no one company can hope to stem the tide of inflation alone, it can take steps to reduce the impact and the cost of inflation by reducing the cost of doing business. Nor does this rather obvious conclusion imply the usual belt tightening in the form of arbitrary reductions in overhead expenses or the customary trimming the fat off the operating accounts. Good management will normally control the appropriate *levels* of such costs and expenses, and any precipitate action by way of arbitrary reductions and layoffs is usually self-defeating in the long run. A more useful approach will be found in examining the structure of the business itself, in challenging not so much the levels of cost as *the basic need for the existence of certain of the cost elements themselves.* And since the management of profit is in its fullest sense the management of capital employed in the business, the logical place to start is with the cost of the capital tied up.

Cost of Capital Employed

The cost of capital used in business is the rate of return that is required in operating profits which will satisfy the assumption of risk by the investor. Historically, and prior to any serious onset of inflation, an adequate rate of return on total capital employed in the average industrial risk has been viewed as a minimum of 10% after taxes, or approximately 20% at the pretax level. This, however, was considered acceptable when the prime rate for bank loans held at a level of around 6%, a spread which gave recognition to the obvious difference in risk between the two types of investment. Inflation, however, will exert an upward pressure on the cost of money, sooner or later pushing the prime rate back up to the 1974 level of 12 percent or higher, with the result that the required rate of return on capital will be leveraged up in a continuing spread in the level of risk at which the funds are employed. And while no precise measurements of risk and rate of return are perhaps available, it would be a safe assumption, and a conservative one, to place the probable cost of risk capital under these conditions at no less than a 15 percent rate of return after taxes or at a pretax level of approximately 30 cents on each dollar of capital employed. Capital thus has a substantial cost, and any idle or nonproductive capital a cost which should not be allowed to continue even under normal economic conditions, and which under inflation clearly cannot be tolerated.

The management of capital rests with the management of the several business assets provided by the capital, and substantial reductions in the cost of doing business are frequently available from a simple review of the *use of assets* in the business—what they represent in terms of money invested, what the levels should be, and what steps are indicated for a possible reduction in asset investment—and hence for a direct reduction in cost. The use of asset investment in business is best measured by relating it to the level of the dollar volume of sales which the assets support, by the measurement of asset turnover found in dividing the average investment into the annual sales volume. And the adequacy of the turnover rates, in turn, is perhaps best tested by comparison with norms or averages found in similar types of business, a comparison which provides a useful bench mark to indicate a probable excess or deficiency in the use of capital.

Table 1

Use of Capital

	Average Balance	*Turnover Rate on $1 Million Sales*
Cash	$ 50,000	20.0
Receivables	200,000	5.0
Inventory	250,000	4.0
Plant and Equipment	200,000	5.0
Miscellaneous Assets	100,000	10.0
Total Assets	$800,000	1.3
Operating Debt	(100,000)	(10.0)
Capital Employed	$700,000	1.4

A typical example of idle capital and hence of excess cost can be seen in Table 1, which analyzes the use of capital in an average manufacturing business. As the table shows, this company is using an average investment of $700,000 in capital to support $1 million in annual sales volume, turning its capital at a rate of approximately 1.4 times a year. At an assumed pretax cost of 30 cents on the dollar for the use of capital, the company is thus incurring a cost of some $210,000 a year, which must be earned from operations if the business is to show an economic profit by recovering the cost of capital employed. While such a cost is properly defined as an economic cost, it is neither less real nor of lesser consequence than a comparable $210,000 cost for materials or labor or a $210,000 expenditure for supporting overhead expense. In the operating accounts, a reduction of any substantial portion of a $210,000 annual cost might indeed be hard to come by, provided only that normal budgetary controls were already in use and that no such obvious excesses were thus permitted to exist.

A far greater potential for cost reduction—for reducing the cost of doing business—may thus be present in the management of assets, a potential which may become quickly evident when the present use of capital is compared with turnover rates more typical of the average need for the business in question (see Table 2).

The situation pictured in this table is one of the excess use of the working-capital elements of the business, one where the presence of idle capital is found more frequently than in the fixed asset investment in plant and equipment, where idle capacity is usually quite obvious. And not only are the working-capital elements the more frequent cause of idle funds, they are also much more susceptible to corrective action in the short term.

Taking each of these elements in turn will indicate the amount of reduction required as well as some typical steps which might be taken for implementation. Excess cash, for example, is a drain on operations, an added level of investment which is clearly nonproductive and which must therefore be supported by other income-producing assets. Idle cash may be present in the cash

Table 2

Turnover Rates

	Turnover Rates		Excess Capital Used
	Actual	*Normal*	
Cash	20.00	40.00	$ 25,000
Receivables	5.0	8.0	75,000
Inventory	4.0	6.0	85,000
Plant and Equipment	5.0	5.0	—
Miscellaneous Assets	10.0	10.0	—
Total Assets	1.3	1.7	$185,000
Operating Debt	(10.0)	(8.7)	15,000
Capital Employed	1.4	2.0	$200,000

account itself, or may be found in the use of cash diverted to investments in marketable securities such as treasury bills. On the assumption that the total funds have not been simply built up to meet a specific planned expenditure over the near term, the modest return which may be realized on such cash investments falls far short of a required 30 cents on the dollar—and in fact represents an actual loss of capital if allowed to continue. The corrective action indicated here is an obvious one; that is, if the cash cannot be put to work in the business it should be returned to the investor, either by paying off any existing bank loans or by having the company buy back some of its own shares on the open market. And if neither of these two options seems available, the use of idle cash in the form of increased dividends to the shareholder would be preferable to continued overinvestment.

In similar fashion, capital tied up in notes and accounts receivable from customers beyond the credit period stipulated by the terms of sale represents, in effect, a source of free capital which the company is providing to its own trade accounts, capital which is clearly not paid for in the normal price of goods and services provided. And even in those cases where interest is charged on past-due balances, the rate of recovery is again far short of the economic need of a 30% return on the funds employed, a situation which also results in a further loss of capital itself. In the example given, a turnover rate of 5 times a year on the money tied up in receivables represents an average collection period of some 72 days as compared with the more normal average of 45 days indicated by an 8 times turn of the investment. The action to be taken here is obvious: either to collect the receivables on time, to charge a full 30% interest rate on past-due balances, or to raise prices high enough to cover the use of the money. Of the three, the added emphasis on collection of the receivables will generally present the most workable solution.

A more difficult problem will usually be found in the management of inventories, a favorite target for asset reduction but one which is seldom put in proper perspective. The measured need for an $85,000 reduction to accomplish a 6 times turn at the present volume of sales is the first step required in the management of funds committed to the inventory account. But the decisions for implementing the reduction must depend upon a detailed review of the several elements of inventory investment. And these decisions may well be shaped by a more thorough understanding of the true cost of carrying the inventory. In addition to a basic cost of 30% a year for the capital tied up, investment in inventory also incurs a series of operating costs for purchasing, receiving, handling, storage, insurance, taxes, and obsolescence—factors which normally account for another 20% in additional costs. When thus seen as having a total carrying cost of some 50% a year, the impact of any possible reductions in inventory will frequently generate its own solutions.

Finally, in the management of working capital, the management of operating debt will provide opportunities for cost reduction which are perhaps the most frequently overlooked. The term *operating debt* refers to the total of all non-interest-bearing obligations of the company, debt which is incurred simply as a byproduct of operations. Chief among these will be the accounts payable to trade creditors, payables for goods and services purchased which might normally carry with them terms of 30 days for the settlement of accounts. And since the use of the supplier's capital for the 30-day period has already been charged in the price to be paid, the proper management of operating debt is to make full use of the funds provided from this source—in short, by not paying such bills before they are due. The probable prepayment of such accounts in the example given is also measured by the turnover rate, where a comparison with more normal averages indicates that payables might be extended by $15,000—an effective reduction in the net amount of capital employed.

In total, the illustration suggests a potential $200,000 reduction in the use of capital, a step which would result in a reduction of $60,000 a year in the cost of doing business at a 30% annual cost rate. This would then represent a reduction of $60,000 that need not be made in operating expenses, or an increase of comparable amount that could be avoided in a higher selling price for the product. Effective action in the management of capital is thus seen as effectively reducing cost as an offset to the impact of inflation on the operating income of the business.

Cost of Operations

In next considering the cost of operations as a target for cost reduction—as a means of reducing the cost of inflation—effective action must be focused on *the need for the existence of the various cost elements of the business* and not dissipated in attempts to squeeze out savings across the board which could well achieve no more than an overall weakening of the business structure itself. In practice, many elements of cost have typically been taken for granted or simply allowed to take root over the years. They must be challenged as to their need and their effectiveness in terms of what they produce in income for the money spent.

Taken in the order in which they are generally presented on the income statement, the first group of cost elements to be challenged would be in the area of discounts and allowances, the segment of cost representing the difference between gross sales and net sales. And one of the prime targets in this area would be the item of cash discounts on sales, a cost which is at least intended as payment for the early collection of receivables. With typical terms of 2% 10 days, net 30, the company is in effect offering a 2% payment for the use of money 20 days in advance of its normal terms, a rate that amounts to an interest charge of 36% a year for the use of cash. Not only is such an interest rate prohibitive in itself, but the device of paying a cash discount seldom works as intended in the first place. In practice, it will be found that many discounts are taken well beyond the discount period allowed, which effectively increases the true interest rate paid on the funds received. It also places the company in the position of simply accepting the result, which many companies do, or of charging back the unearned discount and thus entering into a dispute with its own customers.

Although perhaps originally intended as a payment for the prompt settlement of accounts, cash discount thus frequently degenerates into no more than a net reduction in price—and an awkward one at that, since it involves additional clerical and collection efforts and is by no means administered equitably to all accounts. In essence, it does not work as intended and as a consequence is finding a diminishing use in business in general. Elimination of cash discount is effectively a price increase, but one which is often easier to impose since it does not change the listed price of the product and hence has a lower degree of visibility in the pricing structure. With the need to counter the effects of inflation in every direction possible, the elimination of this cost element may be both one of the most immediate forms of cost reduction available and the easiest to manage.

In the same group of deductions from gross sales will also be found the costs of volume discounts and rebates, costs which have been accepted in efforts to build sales but which frequently prove to be less than profitable when their full impact on earnings is examined in detail. Here it is not uncommon to find discounts of 10% or more given on large orders or as rebates on cumulative annual volume—discounts granted with little or no cost measurement or profit evaluation. As in the case of cash discounts, volume discounts and allowances should be challenged and carefully measured. And in making such an analysis, the effect that such discounts have on *incremental profit* should be weighted against the impact that the resulting volume has on the need for *incremental capital.* Although the rate of the former will almost certainly decline, the rate for the use of capital just as certainly will not. The profitability of volume discounts, in short, rests with their final effect on the net rate of return on capital employed, and in many cases companies would be well advised to forgo the last few increments of volume in favor of a substantial saving in cost.

In next turning to the area of cost of goods sold on the income statement, both the level and the cost content of manufacturing cost may offer fertile ground for a reevaluation of concepts and methods, opportunities for cost reduction which may not have been evident or even available until driven to that point by the pressures of inflation. And while the production costs of most manufacturing operations may have been under a system of close measurement and control for some time past, it is not in the areas of operating efficiency such as labor productivity or materials utilization that substantial savings may now be found, but rather *in a reassessment of the values used,* in a new look at the basic structure of the operation itself.

A new study in terms of value analysis in the design of the product, the type of material components used, and the method of production may serve to highlight areas of cost which were previously considered acceptable but which inflation has now pushed beyond economic limits. Longer production runs may now be indicated; specifications have to be reexamined in the light of what the market will now pay for value added in production; and low-volume items or special runs become candidates for elimination. Inflated costs do not necessarily produce inflated values, and efforts to reduce costs in this particular area could well serve to bring the relationship of value and cost closer to an economic balance.

For companies whose production costs also have a high labor content—the labor-intensive type of businesses—the cost of labor used in production is certainly higher than it was, and just as certainly will go higher still as inflation exerts a continuing upward pressure on wage demands. And since it will not be possible to hold the *rates* of wages down, the only alternative must be to take steps to hold down the effective *cost* of labor used in operations. Here again, the usual approaches of better supervision, improved working conditions, higher morale, and incentive payments for increased productivity all have upward limits which are quickly reached, often leaving the result well short of the desired target and open to a widening gap as the pace continues. Little if any real gains, in short, may be expected of renewed attempts at substantial cost reduction by improving the overall productivity of labor. A new look, instead, should be given to the possibility of *eliminating* much of the cost of labor as a cost element in the business, to changing the method and the value system of the operating structure.

Where labor has been a major element of cost, most companies have looked from time to time at the possibility of mechanization or even complete automation. When labor itself was relatively cheap by comparison, the economics of investment in machinery and equipment required to replace manual operations may have been unattractive and ruled out as too expensive, with the projected rate of return too low to warrant the use of added capital. Conditions, however, have changed, and a new look may well be in order. The cost of machinery and equipment is certainly higher than it was, but so is the cost of labor—and of the two the latter is apt to increase even faster in the future. Capital investment to replace labor may also have a twofold effect on cost—once in the initial savings in method of operation, and again, in the higher quality of output normally found in the mechanized process. The trade-off between the added cost of investment and the reduced cost of operations is not difficult to compute, and for companies with the potential for such a move the plain mathematics of the situation should speak for itself.

Further opportunities for reducing the cost impact of inflation will next be found in a review of the overhead expenses—again, not with the expectation of simply trimming the budget for each department, but with a view to reexamining the need for the existence of the function or department itself. Many cost centers have come into being in a business to meet a particular need of the moment. The need passes, but the function continues or even expands, as Parkinson's law has so convincingly shown. Cost reduction here involves the possible elimination of entire functions or whole departments, moves which not only shut off the flow of unnecessary funds but often have a salutary effect on the rest of the organization as well.

In summary, the attack on the cost of operations, to be effective, must be a measured attack on the structure of the business itself. It can be made to produce often dramatic results in the financial sense while also producing a refreshing change by merely simplifying the mounting problems of business management.

Cost of Products and Markets

In his book *The Great Executive Dream,* Robert Heller proposes the tenth truth of management as: "The easiest way of making money is to stop losing it." And while few managers would be inclined to disagree with the economics of such a statement, they might also find it difficult to know where the losses were taking place. The steps taken thus far should uncover many of them, but other losses—often quite substantial ones—may still remain and be hidden from view.

Obvious losses in terms of the unnecessary cost elements existing in a business, as well as the losses that are perhaps concealed by an inadequate method of accounting, can be brought to light by what amounts to a two-dimensional review of the financial statements, by examining the length and breadth of the balance sheet and the statement of operations. This gives a view of the business as though it were a single operating entity, one with all costs and supporting assets aimed in a single direction and serving one common purpose. In practice, most companies exist as a single entity only in the sense of incorporation, an entity under which a multitude of diverse operations are carried on with respect to products, markets, and methods of distribution. What is needed, then, as a final step in the search for cost reduction is the uncovering of hidden losses, a third-dimensional look at the business. And a third-dimensional look involves the measurement not only of the adequacy of the various elements of cost but the manner in which they are put to work in the business, a measurement not only of the level of assets invested but the manner in which they are deployed in producing income.

A measurement of this kind entails regrouping the financial elements of the business, bringing together the various segments of income, expense, and investment which pertain to a particular product, a single market, or a measurable channel of distribution—in whatever form required to measure the activities of the business, not as the sum of the parts, but as individual entities having strengths and weaknesses of their own.

Product Costs

The first and most obvious measurement of the profitability of the segments of a business will usually be found in the analysis of product or product-line profitability, an analysis whose necessary measurements are typically available from subsidiary records or from a brief review of the identity of the various accounts themselves. The analysis would include, for example, the measurement of sales, the measurement of discounts and allowances, and the direct variable cost of goods sold, as well as a determination of those elements of supporting overhead expenses whose existence is attributable solely to the activity to be measured—elements which when combined would reveal the level of profit contribution provided by the product. The analysis would then also include a typical measurement of inventory investment by product as well as certain identifiable portions of the investment in machinery and equipment required to support production.

In using such an approach, a statement of product profitability might then take the form shown in Table 3 in a company with $1 million in annual sales and $500,000 in average capital employed—a company whose cost of capital has been placed at a rate of 30% a year before taxes.

The analysis in Table 3 reveals, in a series of steps, the unfolding measurement of product profitability—a measurement which frequently changes direction as additional elements are added to the structure. The first level of the measurement of profitability is that of the gross margin on sales, the variable level of income on volume. At this level Product A, with a P/V or profit-to-volume ratio of 50%, shows the highest rate of marginal income and might therefore have been judged to be the most profitable product of the company.

When the next step is added, however, the assignable elements of fixed overhead needed to support the production and sales of Product A alone are seen as consuming all but $10,000 of the margin from sales, thus shifting the measurement of profitability at this level from Product A to Product B, which carries a rate of profit contribution of 30% to sales at the current level of volume.

The final measurement of product profitability, however, does not emerge until the dollars of profit contribution from operations are also linked with the dollar level of asset investment required to support the product-line activity. In this final step the measurement of profitability shifts once more to Product C, where the lower rates of gross margin and of profit contribution to sales are more than offset by a considerably lower need for asset investment. When fully measured in terms of the *rate of return on assets managed,* Product C is thus identified as clearly the most profitable of the three product lines of the business.

The measurement thus establishes the relative profitability of each of the three product lines of the

Table 3

Statement of Product Profitability

	Product A	Product B	Product C	Total
Gross Sales	$100,000	$400,000	$500,000	$1,000,000
Sales Deductions	15,000	25,000	40,000	80,000
Net Sales	$ 85,000	$375,000	$460,000	$ 920,000
Direct Cost of Goods Sold	35,000	195,000	260,000	490,000
Gross Margin	$ 50,000	$180,000	$200,000	$ 430,000
P/V Ratio	50.0%	45.0%	40.0%	43.0%
Assignable Fixed Costs:				
Manufacturing	$ 20,000	$ 20,000	$ 20,000	$ 60,000
Selling	20,000	40,000	80,000	140,000
Total	$ 40,000	$ 60,000	$100,000	$ 200,000
Profit Contribution	$ 10,000	$120,000	$100,000	$ 230,000
% to Sales	10.0%	30.0%	20.0%	23.0%
Assets Managed:				
Inventory	$ 90,000	$ 85,000	$ 75,000	$ 250,000
Equipment	10,000	45,000	25,000	80,000
Total	$100,000	$130,000	$100,000	$ 330,000
Turnover Rate	1.0	3.1	5.0	3.0
Return on Assets Managed	10.0%	93.0%	100.0%	70.0%
Nonassignable Fixed Costs				$ 100,000
Pretax Operating Profit				$ 130,000
Cost of Capital @ 30%				150,000
Pretax Loss				$ (20,000)

company, with each fully measured as to income, expense, and the use of capital. It also provides in this example, as it frequently will in many actual cases, a new insight into the cost of doing business, a picture of an area of economic loss which may not have been apparent before. Since a 70% pretax rate of return on assets managed for total company operations results in an economic loss of $20,000 for the business as a whole, it is obvious that a rate of return of anything less than 70% for any one product also represents an inadequate return and a drain on the business. In this example, the 10% return shown for Product A also results in an economic loss—exactly $20,000 short of the 30% cost of the $100,000 in assets tied up by the product line, a factor contributing directly to the entire loss on capital for the company. It represents, in short, a cost of operations which should be reduced or eliminated as one more step in reducing the cost of inflation. And on the assumption that no basic changes in the present structure of volume, price, cost, or investment for the product were attainable, results for the company would thus be improved by $20,000 a year by dropping the product line and liquidating the investment—*in spite of the fact that it is showing "black ink" in the sense of contributing $10,000 a year in support of common overhead.* Capital has a cost as well, and no operation can be considered profitable until all costs are recovered, including the cost of capital employed.

While the measurement of profitability by product line has thus uncovered one further possibility for cost reduction, others may still exist in the areas of marketing and distribution—costs which are also hidden from view until examined in a similar third-dimensional look. A second view of the company, this time in a measure-

Table 4

Profitability by Channels of Distribution

	Dealer	Consumer	Total
Gross Sales	$400,000	$600,000	$1,000,000
Discounts	68,000	12,000	80,000
Net Sales	$332,000	$588,000	$ 920,000
Direct Cost of Goods Sold	187,000	303,000	490,000
Gross Margin	$145,000	$285,000	$ 430,000
P/V Ratio	36.2%	47.5%	43.0%
Assignable Fixed Costs:			
Selling	—	$140,000	$ 140,000
Profit Contribution	$145,000	$145,000	$ 290,000
% to Sales	36.2%	24.2%	29.0%
Assets Managed:			
Accounts Receivable	$ 85,000	$ 75,000	$ 160,000
Turnover Rate	4.7	8.0	6.2
Return on Assets Managed	170.0%	193.0%	181.0%
Nonassignable Fixed Costs			$ 160,000
Pretax Operating Profit			$ 130,000
Cost of Capital @ 30%			150,000
Pretax Loss			$ (20,000)

ment by channels of distribution, might next disclose the information shown in Table 4.

This second look at the way the elements of cost are put to work in the business and the manner in which assets are deployed in producing income will necessitate a change in the nature of the elements which are subject to measurement. In measuring the profitability of the channels of distribution, as between sales to dealers and sales to consumers, the previously assignable fixed manufacturing costs by product must be left behind and now treated as nonassignable common overhead since all products are assumed to be sold in both markets.

And in similar fashion, the measurement of assets managed will now shift to accounts receivable as the only measurable base of investment, with inventory and equipment assets now also providing common support to the two methods of distribution.

In this analysis it will be seen that the bulk of the variable marketing cost for discounts on sales is attributable to the volume done through dealers, while the entire assignable sales expense of $140,000 is in support of the company-managed consumer sales volume. While the dollars of profit contribution are indeed equally divided between the two, the higher percentage rate of contribution on dealer sales is more than offset by a typically lower turnover or longer collection period for the receivables, one where terms of 60 days may be customary as opposed to the 30-day terms normally given on direct sales.

Since the measurable asset base has been confined to receivables alone, the required rate of return on assets managed is now considerably higher than that found in the measurement of profitability by product line. In this view of operations, a pretax return of 181% on accounts receivable again results in an economic loss of $20,000 for the company, a measurement which again reveals the inadequacy of a return at a lower rate—in this case the rate of return on the business done through dealers. Unlike the situation found for product A, however, the dealer volume is not operating at an economic loss since the level of profit contribution is more than adequate to support a cost of 30% for the assets employed. It emerges simply as the weaker of the two channels of distribution, falling short of the return required to fully support the activity. Corrective action here would then be centered around discounts and terms of sale

Table 5

Relative Profitability by Consumer Sales Region

	East	West	Total
Gross Sales	$200,000	$400,000	$600,000
Discounts	4,000	8,000	12,000
Net Sales	$196,000	$392,000	$588,000
Direct Cost of Goods Sold	96,000	207,000	303,000
Gross Margin	$100,000	$185,000	$285,000
P/V Ratio	50.0%	46.3%	47.5%
Assignable Fixed Costs:			
Selling	$ 40,000	$100,000	$140,000
Profit Contribution	$ 60,000	$ 85,000	$145,000
% to Sales	30.0%	21.3%	24.2%
Assets Managed:			
Accounts Receivable	$ 35,000	$ 40,000	$ 75,000
Turnover Rate	5.7	10.0	8.0
Return on Assets Managed	171.0%	213.0%	193.0%

—areas which provide opportunities for cost reduction which are just as effective as a reduction in overhead expense or an increase in the price of the product itself.

A final measurement of this type might then be found in a further breakdown of the relative profitability of the consumer sales total as between, for example, two sales regions—east and west. This measurement would tie in with the figures already developed and would perhaps reveal even further possibilities for profit improvement, as can be seen in Table 5.

Here, it is found that sales in the eastern region have a somewhat more profitable mix of product volume than in the West, as indicated by the higher rate of marginal income on sales at a P/V ratio of 50%. A further edge in operating profitability is also seen in the second step of measurement, with a correspondingly lower need for supporting selling expenses carrying down to a considerable spread in the rate of profit contribution to sales at 30% for the eastern region. This advantage, however, is again dissipated in the slower collection of receivables, bringing the final measurement of return on assets down to 171% as compared with a rate of 213% in the West. Corrective action for effective cost reduction then narrows down to one of a better management of receivables in the eastern sales region—one where attainment of the 10 times turnover achieved in the western region would reduce receivables by a total of $15,000 for a net saving of $4,500 a year at an annual cost rate of 30% for assets employed.

In summary, opportunities for cost reduction as an effective means of offsetting the impact of inflation exist in many directions in the average business. The more obvious ones will be found in a review of the levels of cost and in challenging the need for various functions and cost elements of the business. Those which are not so obvious, however, will be found only in a third-dimensional look at the operating segments themselves—a look which can yield profit possibilities which may serve to reduce the final need for raising price as a means of inflation management.

12

Pricing
Under Inflation

PRICING has always been one of the most critical areas of business decisions—and one of the most poorly managed. Companies go to great lengths to develop plans and budgets and to install often elaborate systems of measurement and control over costs and expenses, and a few even extend these efforts into the areas of capital investment and the use of turnover rates to measure the level of assets employed in the business. Much is done, in other words, to bring all of the various elements of input to the point of fruition, the point where all of the time and effort, all of the cost and investment incurred, is being offered to the marketplace in the form of a finished product. And at this point all systems and controls, all financial measurements, are literally cast aside in the final process of pricing—a process where all of the preceding measurements are virtually thrown away in a haphazard approach of snap judgments and decisions.

Cost accounting systems may have been developed at considerable effort and expense, systems which provided a viable means of cost measurement and control both by element of cost and by product or product group. Supporting levels of fixed overhead and asset investment may also have been carefully measured as part of the accounting process or information system, with all aspects brought together into a series of meaningful reports and analyses of profitability. The entire structure of financial management, in short, may have been well planned and properly conceived—but is seldom used in the one area where it counts the most.

Where the accumulation of recorded cost data is used for pricing, it is generally subjected to an arbitrary formula that adds a certain percentage to cover general and administrative expenses and to provide a markup for profit. And more often than not, the targeted profit rate assumes that 10% on sales before taxes is the proper objective for all products at all levels of volume—regardless of substantial differences normally existing from product to product in the levels of support required in operating cost and investment. And even this offhand assumption of the pricing need is then frequently discarded in favor of *meeting competition,* a process involving a cursory review of reported information on supposedly competitive prices appearing in the marketplace. The final price then decided upon for the product is next loosely based on a further structure of terms and discounts, a structure which in turn has a major effect on the overall profitability of the product but which is often viewed as mere tactical support of a pricing strategy.

In the long run, the marketplace will indeed set the effective price for any product as long as the competitive system of free enterprise is allowed to function. In the so-called perfect market, prices will adjust to a level which allows for the recovery of all necessary costs, a level which reflects the value added in the process of production and which therefore recognizes the cost of supporting technology as well as the use and cost of capital investment. And while perfect markets seldom exist, the available evidence suggests that they at least tend to move in this direction rather than away from it, and that pricing decisions which deal with such concepts have a greater chance of success in terms of ultimate profitability than those which ignore it.

Since profit is the focal point of business management, pricing must be aimed at producing a profit—not in the manner just described, but on a measured basis calculated to yield the required rate of return on capital invested. And if a proper judgment and control over costs and expenses has been coupled with a proper use of accounting measurements, and if the use of capital has resulted in a proper deployment in the form of supporting assets, then pricing itself becomes the final step in the management of profit. The sequence is fundamentally true under normal economic conditions, but under increasing rates of inflation it may become vital to business survival itself.

Pricing for profit must start with a specific measurement of the rate of profit to be achieved. This rate must be expressed as the required percentage rate of return on invested capital that will satisfy the level of risk at which the capital has been employed. In short, pricing must achieve a rate of return that will recover not only all the measurable supporting costs of operations, but the cost of supporting capital as well. And since total capital seldom supports a single product in the average business, the required rate of return on capital must be translated into the corresponding rate of return on assets managed required for the product or product line. Starting from this base, the typical approach to financial measurement is then inverted, working backward step by step from investment to rate of return, from rate of return to profit contribution, and from profit contribution back to the price required to yield the end result. The process must then be repeated at various levels of volume and capacity, levels which will include changing increments of both cost and investment, levels which will dictate the price required to provide a constant rate of return at various steps in the utilization of productive capacity.

Prices arrived at in this manner will be the exact prices required by the business to yield the objective profit rate of return, but will not necessarily be the prices to be used. Competitive prices in the marketplace must, when fully evaluated in connection with terms and discounts, be a final determining factor in the pricing decision. The method proposed, that of pricing for a specific measurable rate of profit, quite obviously does not become an automatic tool which will replace or do away with the final process of judgment required by management. What it will provide, however, is a somewhat precise measurement of what the price should be as well as a clearly visible projection of how a deviation from such a price will affect the profitability of the

Table 6. Return on Assets Managed (ROAM)

Manufacturing Direct	.25 Capacity			.35 Capacity		
	$	P.C.	Turns	$	P.C.	Turns
Direct Material	179	.38		250	.42	
Hourly Labor	22	.05		31	.05	
Variable Burden	27	.06		38	.06	
Other Direct						
Total Mfg. Direct	228	.48		319	.53	
C.O.P.	245	.52		282	.47	
Assignable Selling						
Commissions	5	.01		7	.01	
Royalty-Warranty						
Cash Discount	6	.01		9	.01	
Promotion-Adv.						
Other						
Total Selling	11	.02		16	.03	
Total Cost	239	.51		335	.56	
Gross Margin	234	.49		266	.44	
Assets Managed						
Finished Goods	101	.21	4.68	106	.18	5.67
Raw & Semi-Fin.	53	.11	8.92	56	.09	10.73
Work in Process						
Total Inventory	154	.33	3.07	162	.27	3.71
Accounts Rec.	71	.15	6.66	94	.16	6.39
Equipment						
Total Assets	225	.48	2.10	256	.43	2.35
Net Sales Required	473			601		
Volume Discount	22			28		
Gross Sales	495			629		
ROAM	104			104		

XYZ Manufacturing Co.

.45 Capacity			.55 Capacity			.65 Capacity		
$	P.C.	Turns	$	P.C.	Turns	$	P.C.	Turns
321	.43		393	.44		464	.45	
40	.05		49	.05		58	.06	
49	.07		60	.07		71	.07	
410	.55		502	.56		593	.57	
331	.45		391	.44		444	.43	
9	.01		11	.01		13	.01	
12	.02		14	.02		17	.02	
21	.03		25	.03		30	.03	
431	.58		527	.59		623	.60	
310	.42		366	.41		414	.40	
121	.16	6.12	144	.16	6.20	163	.16	6.36
61	.08	12.15	69	.08	12.94	76	.07	13.64
182	.25	4.07	213	.24	4.19	239	.23	4.34
116	.16	6.39	139	.16	6.42	159	.15	6.52
298	.40	2.49	352	.39	2.54	398	.38	2.61
741			893			1037		
35			42			49		
776			935			1086		
104			104			104		

operation. It will provide, in short, a standard of pricing performance as a bench mark or point of departure from which pricing judgments can be made with full knowledge of their impact on the business.

But once again, while the method thus described will work and work well—and indeed has already been adopted in many companies—the impact of continuing inflation will impose special needs upon the system, needs to keep abreast of the changing values of both cost and investment, needs to project the level of future prices based on anticipated future costs. These needs have not only already been foreseen by one particular company, but have already been met by a planned approach to pricing under inflation.

A Systems Approach

The systems approach to pricing and the sample computer printouts which follow are in actual use in a company where the author has served as a financial consultant, and are presented with the full knowledge and consent of the client with the obvious stipulation that all references to company name and product identification be deleted.

The first step taken was to review the levels of all costs and related investment to insure that no excess costs were built into the planned pricing structure. This was followed by a series of third-dimensional measurements of profitability such as previously described, with the objective in this case quite obviously one of product-line requirements. Capacity was next determined as the output available from normal two-shift operations based on a five-day workweek, with prices to be determined at five different levels of capacity ranging up to a level of 65% based on a plan to optimize profitability at approximately two-thirds of rated capacity. Finally, an analysis was made which determined that a rate of return on assets managed of 104% pretax, a measurement abbreviated as ROAM in the system, would be required to reach the profit target for one particular product group. And since the size and complexity of operations indicated the value of a computerized approach, the various inputs were then programmed to provide for the calculation of selling prices required at the various levels of capacity. This was accomplished by computing the net dollar volume of sales required to meet the target, with pricing for each individual product type within the group to be based on the relationship of total direct manufacturing cost to sales. A computer printout of this first calculation for one of many product groups was then produced in the form shown in Table 6.

The measurements provided by this report produced, in effect, no more than a single set of figures to be carried forward to the next—and more complex—use of the measurement as a pricing tool. Since all the measurable elements of cost and asset investment were now fully accounted for, including those selling expenses which were attributable solely to the product group in question, the technique for pricing could now be condensed to a single ratio: the percentage of direct manufacturing cost to sales. This percentage could then be divided, in turn, into the unit direct cost of any one product type in the group to establish the desired selling price. For this particular product group the ratios as computed were as follows:

	Percent of Direct Manufacturing
Percent of Capacity	*Cost to Sales*
25%	48%
35	53
45	55
55	56
65	57

With a constant unit cost of production—a value independent of the effect of volume under a system of direct costing—the increasing percentage of direct manufacturing cost to selling price would, in other words, indicate a decreasing level of prices required at progressively higher levels of capacity and volume.

The next step was to apply these ratios to individual product types within the product group in the form of a selling price study. This was also done on the computer, but in a step which also added further inputs in the form of anticipated cost increases for labor and materials, and in variable overhead expenses projected in each of the ensuing months. Price-to-cost ratios were then applied at four preselected points in time and at different levels of volume, providing in advance for planned price increases (or decreases where indicated by the possibility of higher volume) as of January 30, March 1, May 1, and September 1 of the calendar year.

A second computer printout using these additional inputs was next produced on a trial basis, showing prices currently in use together with computed prices to be used in May and in September based on the estimates given. A portion of that printout for eight product types within the group showed the results to be seen in Table 7.

Table 7

Selling Price Study

Cat. No.	—Selling Price—				Fcast	Jan	Feb	Mar	Apr	May	Jun	Jul	Aug	Sep	Oct	Nov	Dec
	1/30	3/1	5/1	9/1													
2523	8.20	8.20	9.29	9.29		4.643	4.687	4.731	4.820	4.922	5.010	5.054	5.098	5.142	5.187	5.831	5.231
3576	9.40	9.40	10.50	10.50		5.250	5.300	5.351	5.432	5.565	5.666	5.717	5.767	5.817	5.868	5.918	5.918
2998	11.75	11.75	14.39	14.39		7.193	7.262	7.330	7.468	7.626	7.764	7.833	7.901	7.870	8.039	8.107	8.107
1127	12.90	12.90	12.10	12.10		6.053	6.109	6.165	6.278	6.414	6.527	6.583	6.639	6.696	6.752	6.808	6.806
959	17.70	17.70	17.60	17.60		8.830	8.895	8.960	0.090	9.328	9.458	9.523	9.588	9.653	9.718	9.783	9.783
4140	23.55	23.55	22.12	22.12		11.078	11.160	11.242	11.406	11.721	11.885	11.987	12.049	12.131	12.213	12.294	12.294
2843	20.65	20.65	18.52	18.52		9.235	9.316	9.397	9.688	9.816	9.977	10.058	10.139	10.219	10.300	10.381	10.381
915	10.55	10.55	13.28	13.28		6.640	6.706	6.771	6.906	7.038	7.171	7.238	7.304	7.370	7.437	7.503	7.508

This study showed first of all that the existing prices of exactly half the product types within the group—four out of eight—had been set too low and should be increased on the next planned date of May 1. It also showed, interestingly enough, that the remaining four types had been priced too high and could be reduced at the same time, a factor that would thus result in an overall readjustment of prices to be announced for this product group rather than an across-the-board increase.

The first type in the group, for example, was currently priced at $8.20, but with a predicted unit direct manufacturing cost of $4.92 by the first of May and at a level of volume estimated at a 35% utilization of capacity, a price of $9.29 would be required at the cost/price ratio of 53% indicated by the ROAM analysis previously made. It was also determined that the same price of $9.29 would be sufficient even at the higher unit cost of $5.14 projected for September if the volume could be increased to a level of 45% of capacity, a level where a ratio of 55% of cost to price would still meet the same profit requirement.

The prices thus calculated were, of course, subject to final review and comparison with competitive markets before being adopted. In doing so, however, the company was able to move on pricing with the full knowledge of exactly what was needed on a measured basis to make its pricing decisions with the ready ability to calculate the profit impact of any deviation from target prices that the market might dictate at any one point in time.

When it was thus deemed necessary to follow a lower competitive price on certain product types, for example, the company also had the means to measure the need for a change in product mix as a method of offsetting such lower prices, an effective means of profit management by way of averaging the results.

The program allows for an immediate updating of pricing requirements on receipt of changing cost inputs, so that notice of an announced or projected cost increase in any one element of the structure can be added to the system at once, providing a fast reaction capability in pricing at all times. It also provides a model for pricing simulation, whereby projected or assumed levels of competitive prices can be put into the system and worked back into targeted unit costs of production or targeted levels of supporting fixed overhead or asset investment required to meet such prices and still remain on the desired profit curve.

In essence, the systems approach to pricing which this company has adopted is a program which may be described as highly sophisticated in one sense, but in another is no more than the logical outcome of a series of very basic steps and measurements in the profitable use of financial analysis. It is available to any company that will take the time to work it out, available to any company willing to meet the challenge of management under the changing rules of inflation. As one editorial writer put it quite recently, "it is a time for realism about inflation. Corporate officers can hardly blame politicians for not facing the facts when they themselves are partly to blame for obscuring them."

Index

AMACOM Executive Books-Paperbacks

John D. Arnold	The Art of Decision Making: 7 Steps to Achieving More Effective Results	$6.95
Eugene L. Benge	Elements of Modern Management	$5.95
Alec Benn	The 27 Most Common Mistakes in Advertising	$5.95
Dudley Bennett	TA and the Manager	$6.95
Warren Bennis	The Unconscious Conspiracy	$5.95
Don Berliner	Want a Job? Get Some Experience...	$5.95
Borst & Montana	Managing Nonprofit Organizations	$6.95
J. Douglas Brown	The Human Nature of Organizations	$5.95
Ronald D. Brown	From Selling to Managing	$5.95
Richard E. Byrd	A Guide to Personal Risk Taking	$5.95
Logan Cheek	Zero-Base Budgeting Comes of Age	$6.95
William A. Cohen	The Executive's Guide to Finding a Superior Job	$5.95
Richard R. Conarroe	Bravely, Bravely in Business	$4.95
Ken Cooper	Bodybusiness	$5.95
James J. Cribbin	Effective Managerial Leadership	$6.95
John D. Drake	Interviewing for Managers	$5.95
Richard J. Dunsing	You and I Have Simply Got to Stop Meeting This Way	$5.95
Sidney Edlund	There Is a Better Way to Sell	$5.95
Elam & Paley	Marketing for the Nonmarketing Executive	$5.95
Norman L. Enger	Management Standards for Developing Information Systems	$6.95
Figueroa & Winkler	A Business Information Guidebook	$9.95
Saul W. Gellerman	Motivation and Productivity	$6.95
Roger A. Golde	Muddling Through	$5.95
Bernard Haldane	Career Satisfaction and Success	$5.95
Lois B. Hart	Moving Up! Women and Leadership	$6.95
Hart & Schleicher	A Conference and Workshop Planner's Manual	$15.95
Michael Hayes	Pay Yourself First: The High Beta/No-Load Way to Stock Market Profits	$6.95
Maurice R. Hecht	What Happens in Management	$7.95
Charles L. Hughes	Goal Setting	$5.95
John W. Humble	How to Manage By Objectives	$5.95
Jones & Trentin	Budgeting (rev. ed.)	$12.95
Donald P. Kenney	Minicomputers	$7.95
Ray A. Killian	Managing Human Resources	$6.95
William H. Krause	How to Hire and Motivate Manufacturers' Representatives	$6.95